First World W[...]
and Army of Occupati[...]

GW00370590

War Diary
France, Belgium and Germany

40 DIVISION
120 Infantry Brigade
East Surrey Regiment
13th Battalion
3 June 1916 - 30 January 1918

WO95/2612/3

The Naval & Military Press Ltd
www.nmarchive.com
Published in association with The National Archives

Published by

The Naval & Military Press Ltd

Unit 10 Ridgewood Industrial Park,

Uckfield, East Sussex,

TN22 5QE England

Tel: +44 (0) 1825 749494

www.naval-military-press.com

www.nmarchive.com

Contents

Miscellaneous	Appendix I Report on Minor Operation Carried Out by The 13th Bn East Surrey Regt on The Night of The 29/30th September 1916	01/10/1916	01/10/1916
Miscellaneous	Appendix II. H.2 120th Infantry Brigade.	06/10/1916	06/10/1916
Miscellaneous	Appendix III H.Q. 130th Infantry Brigade. Minor Operation Night 5th/6th Oct 1916		
Heading	War Diary of 13th Bn East Surrey Regt. from Nov. 1st to Nov. 30th 1916		
War Diary	Averdoingt (Departement Pas De Calais)	01/11/1916	02/11/1916
War Diary	Rebreuve	03/11/1916	04/11/1916
War Diary	Mezerolles (Departement De La Somme.)	05/11/1916	05/11/1916
War Diary	Vacquerie	06/11/1916	12/11/1916
War Diary	Doullens	13/11/1916	14/11/1916
War Diary	Souastre	15/11/1916	15/11/1916
War Diary	Hebuterne	16/11/1916	21/11/1916
War Diary	Couin	22/11/1916	22/11/1916
War Diary	Amplier	23/11/1916	23/11/1916
War Diary	Bonneville	24/11/1916	24/11/1916
War Diary	Bussus	25/11/1916	30/11/1916
Miscellaneous	Roll of Officers Serving With the Battalion on 11th November 1916		
Heading	War Diary of 13th Battn East Surrey Regiment Volume 7 1st December 1916-31st December 1916		
War Diary	Bussus	01/12/1916	14/12/1916
War Diary	Pont Remy	15/12/1916	15/12/1916
War Diary	Camp 112	16/12/1916	26/12/1916
War Diary	Bouchavesnes	27/12/1916	31/12/1916
Heading	War Diary of 13th Battalion East Surrey Regiment Volume 8 1st January 1917 to 31st January 1917		
War Diary	Camp 21 Maricourt	01/01/1917	04/01/1917
War Diary	Rancourt	05/01/1917	08/01/1917
War Diary	Maurepas	09/01/1917	12/01/1917
War Diary	Camp 21 Maricourt	13/01/1917	18/01/1917
War Diary	Bouchavesnes North	18/01/1917	22/01/1917
War Diary	Asquith Flats	23/01/1917	27/01/1917
War Diary	Corbie	28/01/1917	31/01/1917
Heading	War Diary of 13th Battalion East Surrey Regiment 1st February 1917 to 28th February 1917 Volume 9		
War Diary	Corbie	01/02/1917	10/02/1917
War Diary	Camp III	11/02/1917	11/02/1917
War Diary	Bray-Tour Biere	12/02/1917	24/02/1917
War Diary	Camp 21	25/02/1917	28/02/1917
Heading	War Diary of 13th Bn East Surrey Regt Volume 10 from 1st March 1917 to 31st March 1917 Vol 10		
War Diary	Camp 21 Maricourt	01/03/1917	06/03/1917
War Diary	Road Wood SW of Bouchavesnes	07/03/1917	07/03/1917
War Diary	Bethune Road	08/03/1917	10/03/1917
War Diary	Howitzer Wood	11/03/1917	13/03/1917
War Diary	Bethune Road	14/03/1917	18/03/1917
War Diary	Road Wood	19/03/1917	19/03/1917
War Diary	Allaines	20/03/1917	20/03/1917
War Diary	Curlu	21/03/1917	30/03/1917
Miscellaneous	Operation Order by Lt Col. W Newton Cmdg 13th Bn E. Surr. Regt.	15/03/1917	15/03/1917
Heading	War Diary of 13th Bn East Surrey Regt Volume 11 from 1st April 1917 to 30th April 1917		

War Diary	Curlu	01/04/1917	16/04/1917
War Diary	Equancourt	17/04/1917	18/04/1917
War Diary	Gouzeaucourt Wood	19/04/1917	24/04/1917
War Diary	Villers Plouich	25/04/1917	25/04/1917
Miscellaneous	List of Officers who went into action on the Morning of the 24th April 1917		
War Diary	Appendix the attack on Villers Flouich	24/04/1917	24/04/1917
War Diary	Villers Plouich	20/04/1917	20/04/1917
War Diary	Equancourt	26/04/1917	30/04/1917
Operation(al) Order(s)	13th Bn East Surrey Regiment Operation Order No. 48	23/04/1917	23/04/1917
Miscellaneous	East Surrey Regt. O.O. 47	20/04/1917	20/04/1917
Heading	War Diary of 13th Bn East Surrey Regt Volume 12 from 1st May 1917 to 31st May 1917 Vol 12		
War Diary	Equancourt	01/05/1917	01/05/1917
War Diary	Queens Cross Near Couzeaucourt	02/05/1917	06/05/1917
War Diary	Villers Plouich	07/05/1917	12/05/1917
War Diary	Sorel	13/05/1917	13/05/1917
War Diary	S of Gouzeau Court.	14/05/1917	18/05/1917
War Diary	Villers Guislain	19/05/1917	25/05/1917
War Diary	Dessert Wood	26/05/1917	26/05/1917
War Diary	Gouzeaucourt	27/05/1917	31/05/1917
Heading	War Diary of 13th Bn East Surrey Regt Volume 14 from 1st June 1917 to 30th June 1917		
War Diary	Gouzeaucourt.	01/06/1917	03/06/1917
War Diary	Gonnelieu Sector	04/06/1917	11/06/1917
War Diary	Dessart Wood	12/06/1917	19/06/1917
War Diary	Villers Plouich Sector	20/06/1917	30/06/1917
Heading	War Diary of 13th Bn East Surrey Regt Volume 14 from 1st July 1917 to 31st July 1917 Vol 14		
War Diary	Villers Plouich Sector	01/07/1917	05/07/1917
War Diary	15 Ravine	06/07/1917	13/07/1917
War Diary	Villers Plouich Sector	14/07/1917	21/07/1917
War Diary	Gouzeaqucourt	22/07/1917	31/07/1917
Miscellaneous	Appendix I Report on Minor Enterprise No. 1 on the Night 20/21st July 1917		
Heading	War Diary of 13th Bn East Surrey Regt Volume 16 from Aug 1st 1917 to Augt 31st 1917		
War Diary	Villers Plouich	01/08/1917	31/08/1917
Heading	13th Battn East Surrey Regt War Diary for Month Ending 30th September 1917 Vol 16		
War Diary	Beaucamp	01/09/1917	07/09/1917
War Diary	Fifteen Ravine	08/09/1917	12/09/1917
War Diary	Beaucamp	13/09/1917	30/09/1917
Heading	War Diary of 13th Bn East Surrey Regt Volume 17. for The Month of October 1917 Vol 17		
War Diary	Beaucamp	01/10/1917	01/10/1917
War Diary	Fifteen Ravine	02/10/1917	05/10/1917
War Diary	Heudecourt (Camp)	06/10/1917	06/10/1917
War Diary	Peronne	07/10/1917	09/10/1917
War Diary	Berneville	10/10/1917	31/10/1917
Heading	War Diary of 13th E Surrey for Nov 1917		
Heading	War Diary of The 13th Bn East Surrey Regt Volume XVIII For The Month of November 1917 Vol 18		
War Diary	Grenas	01/11/1917	16/11/1917
War Diary	Beaneville	17/11/1917	17/11/1917
War Diary	Courcelles Le Comte	18/11/1917	19/11/1917

War Diary	Beaulea Court	20/11/1917	22/11/1917
War Diary	Lebucquere	23/11/1917	24/11/1917
War Diary	Bourlon Wood	24/11/1917	30/11/1917
Miscellaneous	Headquarters, 120th Infantry Brigade.	29/11/1917	29/11/1917
Miscellaneous	To Adjutant 13th East Surrey Regt.		
Miscellaneous	Adjutant Estimated casualty return		
Miscellaneous	121 Inf. Bde.	24/11/1917	24/11/1917
Miscellaneous			
Miscellaneous	O.C. 13th East Surreys.	27/11/1917	27/11/1917
Miscellaneous	To Adjutant 13th East Surrey Regt	26/11/1917	26/11/1917
Miscellaneous	To OC. Bourlon Defences	26/11/1917	26/11/1917
Miscellaneous	Adjutant 13 ESR		
Miscellaneous	O.C. Out Posts.	26/11/1917	26/11/1917
Miscellaneous	Adjutant 13 ESR		
Miscellaneous	Numbers Going into Action		
Miscellaneous	To Lt. Col Warden Comdg East Surrey Regiment	27/11/1917	27/11/1917
Miscellaneous	OC 13th East Surreys	28/04/1917	28/04/1917
Miscellaneous	OC 13th B Sur R		
Miscellaneous	13th Bn East Surrey Regt Casualties		
Miscellaneous	To Adjutant 13th East Surrey Rgt.		
Miscellaneous	A Form. Messages And Signals.		
Miscellaneous	Messages And Signals.		
Miscellaneous	Adjutant Disposition Report Despatched 10.25	25/11/1917	25/11/1917
Miscellaneous	From 121 Bde HQ to OC. 13th E Surreys	25/11/1917	25/11/1917
Miscellaneous	O.C. 14 H.L.I		
Miscellaneous	To Adjutant 13th East Surrey	26/11/1917	26/11/1917
Miscellaneous	Plus 2 Coys 5th K.O.Y.L.I.		
Miscellaneous	Adjt 13th E Surrey Regt.	26/11/1917	26/11/1917
Miscellaneous	Adjt 13th E Surrey Regt.		
Miscellaneous	Adjutant 13th East Surrey Rgt		
Miscellaneous	Adjutant 13th E S R		
Miscellaneous	To Adjutant 13th East Surrey Rgt.	25/11/1917	25/11/1917
Miscellaneous	To Adjutant 13th East Surrey Rgt.	26/11/1917	26/11/1917
Miscellaneous	Adjutant 13th East Surrey Rgt.	26/11/1917	26/11/1917
Miscellaneous	OC 13 E Surrey Rgt.		
Miscellaneous		25/11/1917	25/11/1917
Miscellaneous	To Adjutant 13th East Surrey Rgt.	25/11/1917	25/11/1917
Miscellaneous	To Adjutant 13th East Surrey Rgt.		
Miscellaneous	Adjutant		
Miscellaneous	To Lt Col Warden 13th East Surrey Rgt.	25/11/1917	25/11/1917
Miscellaneous	Adjt 13th E Surrey Regt.	25/11/1917	25/11/1917
Miscellaneous	Adjt B ES		
Miscellaneous	O.C. C.E Capt	25/11/1917	25/11/1917
Miscellaneous	OC D G CD		
Miscellaneous	Adjutant 13th East Surrey		
Miscellaneous	The Commanding Officer 13th East Surreys		
Miscellaneous			
Miscellaneous	Of Tanks	25/11/1917	25/11/1917
Miscellaneous			
Miscellaneous	O.C. 14 H.L.I		
Miscellaneous	O.C. 13 East Surrey Rgt	24/10/1917	24/10/1917
Miscellaneous	Adjutant 13th Bn East Surrey Rgt	25/11/1917	25/11/1917
Miscellaneous	DC A B C D		
Miscellaneous	Adjutant to E 12.d.8.9		
Miscellaneous	O.C. Coys	25/11/1917	25/11/1917
Miscellaneous	O.C. E Surrey Regt		

605am / 2/9/2 (3)

605am / 2/9/2 (3)

13TH BN EAST SURREY REGT

JUN 1916-JAN 1918

To 119 BDE 40DIV

13. East Surrey

Vol I

$\frac{120}{40}$

XL

Original

Confidential

War Diary

of

13th. (Service) Bn. East Surrey Regt.

From 3rd June 1916 to 30th June 1916

(Volume I)

WAR DIARY

or

INTELLIGENCE SUMMARY

(Erase heading not required.)

13TH (Service) BATTALION
EAST SURREY REGIMENT (WANDSWORTH) 120TH INF. BRIGADE
40TH DIVISION.

Instructions regarding War Diaries and Intelligence
Summaries are contained in F. S. Regs, Part II.
and the Staff Manual respectively. Title Pages
will be prepared in manuscript.

Place	Date	Hour	Summary of Events and Information	Remarks and references to Appendices
BLACKDOWN	3.6.16		The Battalion received orders to proceed to FRANCE. The strength of the Battalion was – Officers 33 ; Other Ranks 970. The following is the roll of Officers :–	
			Headquarters :– Lieut-Colonel W.C.NEWTON (Major MIDDLESEX REGT) Comdg. Major F.S.B.JOHNSON (late THE KING'S OWN REGT.) Second-in-Command ; Capt. C.E.LINGE Adjutant ; Lieut. F.FOSTER Quartermaster.	
			A. Company :– Major R.S.TAYLOR ; Capt. E.CROCKER ; Lieut. R.H.HARKER ; T.F.DAVIS ; 2nd Lieut. A.F.SENIOR ; F.W.LANHAM (Bombing Officer) R.W.H.KING.	
			B. Company :– Capt. M.PEMBERTON ; Lieut. C.R.BLACKBURNE ; F.S.AINGER ; 2nd Lieut. A.L.ANDERSON ; J.R.HUCKER (Signalling Officer) L.F.MENZIES–JONES ; W.F.C.EMBLEY.	
			C. Company :– Capt. L.R.MERRYFIELD ; Capt. H.P.NAUNTON ; Lieut. F.J.T.HANN (Machine Gun Officer) ; M.STANFORD ; 2nd Lieut. G.E.HEAD ; V.W.SCOTT (Sniping Officer) ; T.N.HUCKER ; G.K.FIELDING	
			D. Company :– Capt. L.B.MILLS ; Capt. O.G.NORMAN ; Lieut. E.S.BEECROFT (Transport Officer) E.B.BUCKLAND ; F.N.CORBEN ; 2nd Lieut. L.I.DEACON ; G.E.DEACON.	
			Lieut. G.R.SPENCE R.A.M.C. (Medical Officer) No. 3200 R.J.M. E.J.SEYMOUR No. 15614 R.Q.M.J. F.C.WEBB	
			The Battalion entrained at FRIMLEY STATION and proceeded to SOUTHAMPTON in two detachments, the first train (Commanded by Major F.S.B.JOHNSON) Conveying A and B Companies ; and the second train (Commanded by LIEUT-COLONEL W.C.NEWTON)	

1875 Wt. W593/826 1,009,000 4/15 J.B.C. &.A. A.D.S.S./Forms/C. 2118.

Army Form C. 2118

13TH (Service) BATTALION
EAST SURREY REGIMENT (WANDSWORTH) **WAR DIARY**
or
INTELLIGENCE SUMMARY

120TH INF BRIGADE
40TH DIVISION

Instructions regarding War Diaries and Intelligence
Summaries are contained in F. S. Regs., Part II.
and the Staff Manual respectively. Title Pages
will be prepared in manuscript.

(*Erase heading not required.*)

Place	Date	Hour	Summary of Events and Information	Remarks and references to Appendices
BLACKDOWN	3.6.16	etc.	conveying Headquarters, C + D Companies	
SOUTHAMPTON	3.6.16		For the sea-voyage two boats were allotted to the Battalion — The QUEEN ALEXANDRIA and the HUNSCRAFT. In the former travelled Headquarters (less Major JOHNSON) part of A Company, the whole of B + C Companies and part of D Company; in the HUNSCRAFT accommodation was found for the remainder of A Company, part of D Company and the transport. Major JOHNSON commanded the East Surrey detachment on the HUNSCRAFT.	Qn A
HAVRE	4.6.16		After disembarkation each detachment marched to No. 1 REST CAMP where the Battalion was re-united and encamped for the night.	Q A
LILLERS	5.6.16		The Battalion entrained at HAVRE and proceeded by two trains to LILLERS	N A
FANCQUENHEM	6.6.16		The Battalion arrived at LILLERS and marched into billets at LIÈRES and FANCQUENHEM (Note:- The journey from BLACKDOWN to LIÈRES was accomplished without a casualty.) On arrival at FANCQUENHEM it was notified that the 40TH Division of which the Battalion forms part had been allotted to the FIRST CORPS, FIRST ARMY (FIRST ARMY was commanded by Gen'l. Sir C. MONRO GCMG KCB.) A Coy was billetted in LIÈRES and billets for Hqrs., B, C + D Companies were found in FANCQUENHEM. The billets of the Battalion were satisfactory but the drinking water, when examined by the Medical Officer, was found to require treatment — one measure of chloride of lime for the well water and two measures for the water obtained from the stream.	Ref. Map BELGIUM. HAZEBROUCK 5A. OSO. 1915.

1875 Wt. W593/826 1,009,900 4/15 J.B.C. & A. A.D.S.S./Forms/C. 2118.

Army Form C. 2118

WAR DIARY

or

INTELLIGENCE SUMMARY

(Erase heading not required.)

Instructions regarding War Diaries and Intelligence
Summaries are contained in F. S. Regs., Part II. /207TH INF. BRIGADE
and the Staff Manual respectively. Title Pages   40TH DIVISION
will be prepared in manuscript.

Place	Date	Hour	Summary of Events and Information	Remarks and references to Appendices
FANCQUENHEM	6.6.16		Communication was established by means of telephones and cyclists with:- Brigade Headquarters at ECQUEDECQUES v with the Headquarters of the three other Battalions in this Brigade viz. 11th (K.O.) R. Lancs Regt. at LIÈRES 14th Highland Light Infantry at ECQUEDECQUES 4/14th Argyll & Sutherland Highlanders at ECQUEDECQUES	Nil
	7.6.16		The Battalion went for a route march keeping to the pavé as much as possible in order to get the men accustomed to this sort of road.	Nil
	8.6.16		11 men of the 11th (K.O.) R. Lancs Regt. who had been transferred to this Regiment on the 3rd instant & 6 men of the 13th East Surrey Regt. who had come over-seas with the 14th Bn. Argyll & Sutherland Highlanders reported for duty. Route march by Companies	Nil
	9.6.16		Route march by Companies.	Nil
	10.6.16		Orders were received for the Battalion to proceed to SAILLY LA BOURSE on the 15th instant, whence they would be attached to the 44th Infantry Brigade to receive instruction in trench warfare.	Nil
	11.6.16		Brigade Headquarters were transferred from ECQUEDECQUES to BETHUNE Church Parade on Battalion Parade Ground	Nil

1875   Wt. W593/826   1,000,000 4/15 J.B.C. & A.   A.D.S.S./Forms/C. 2118.

13TH (Service) BATTALION
EAST SURREY REGIMENT (WANDSWORTH)

Army Form C. 2118

WAR DIARY
or
INTELLIGENCE SUMMARY

II./20TH INF. BRIGADE
40TH DIVISION

(*Erase heading not required.*)

Instructions regarding War Diaries and Intelligence
Summaries are contained in F. S. Regs., Part II.
and the Staff Manual respectively. Title Pages
will be prepared in manuscript.

Place	Date	Hour	Summary of Events and Information	Remarks and references to Appendices
FANCQUENHEM	12.6.16		The Battalion in co-operation with the 14th (K) Battn. Argyll & Sutherland Highlanders filled in some old trenches at ECQUEDECQUES.	Wt
	13.6.16		A Memorial Service to the late Field Marshal Earl KITCHENER was held on the Battalion Parade Ground. A. Coy. marched by parties of 50 to the baths at AMETTES.	Wt
	14.6.16		B. C. & D. Companies marched by parties of 50 to the baths at AMETTES.	Wt
	15.6.16		The Battalion paraded at 8 hrs. & marched via LILLERS - CHOCQUES - BETHUNE - BEUVRY to SAILLY LA BOURSE. Headquarters A, B & C Companies were billetted at SAILLY LABOURSE and D Company was accommodated in shell proof huts at NOYELLES	Wt
SAILLY LA BOURSE	16.6.16		The Battalion was attached to the 44th Infantry Brigade (occupying trenches in HULLUCH sector) for individual and platoon training. Companies were attached to Battalions as under :- A Company to 8th Battn. Seaforth Highlanders B " " 8/10 " " Gordon Highlanders C " " 7th " " Cameron Highlanders D " " 9th " " Black Watch Two teams of the Lewis Gun Section & four Battalion Signallers were attached	

1875 Wt. W593/826 1,000,000 4/15 J.B.C. &A. A.D.S.S./Forms/C. 2118.

13TH (Service) BATTALION

EAST SURREY REGIMENT (WANDSWORTH)

WAR DIARY
or'
INTELLIGENCE SUMMARY

Army Form C. 2118

Instructions regarding War Diaries and Intelligence
Summaries are contained in F. S. Regs., Part II.
and the Staff Manual respectively. Title Pages
will be prepared in manuscript.

20TH INF. BRIGADE
40TH DIVISION

(Erase heading not required.)

Place	Date	Hour	Summary of Events and Information	Remarks and references to Appendices
SAILLY LA BOURSE	16.6.16	etc.	to each Battalion.	
			The Signalling Officer was attached to the 9th Cameron Hrs. and the Lewis Gun Officer to the 9th Black Watch.	
			Battalion Headquarters were transferred to BETHUNE. The Quartermaster Stores and the Transport remained at SAILLY LA BOURSE.	M.H.
			12715 Pte Mooney H. was wounded by shrapnel.	
BETHUNE	17.6.16		Battalion under instruction in trenches. Casualties - 4 O.R. wounded 1 O.R. sent to hospital suffering from shock.	M.H.
	18.6.16		Battalion under instruction in trenches. Casualties :- 14040 Pte Morris J. killed 3 O.R. wounded 1 O.R. sent to hospital suffering from shock.	M.H.
	19.6.16		Battalion under instruction in trenches. Casualties 4 O.R. wounded (1 of whom died of wounds on 21/6/16.)	M.H.
	20.6.16		The Battalion left the trenches and concentrated at SAILLY LA BOURSE. Headquarters A. B & C (less 1 platoon) were billetted at SAILLY LA BOURSE. D Coy. were billetted in huts at NOYELLES & one platoon of C Coy. were billetted at LABOURSE.	
			Captain A.N.N. DRUMMOND 8/10th Battn. Gordon Highlanders reported as Instructor	

1875 W.: W593/826 1,000,000 4/15 J.B.C. & A. A.D.S.S./Forms/C.2118.

13th (Service) BATTALION
EAST SURREY REGIMENT (WANDSWORTH)

Army Form C. 2

WAR DIARY
or
INTELLIGENCE SUMMARY

(Erase heading not required.)

Instructions regarding War Diaries and Intelligence Summaries are contained in F. S. Regs., Part II. and the Staff Manual respectively. Title Pages will be prepared in manuscript.

120th INF. BRIGADE
40th DIVISION

Place	Date	Hour	Summary of Events and Information	Remarks and references to Appendices
	20.6.16	std.	to the Battalion whilst in rest killed. Casualty 1 O.R. accidentally killed.	JRH
SAILLY LA BOURSE	21.6.16		Arrangements were made for half the Battalion to go to the Baths at LABOURSE. Lectures were given by Capt. DRUMMOND.	RH
	22.6.16		The remainder of the Battalion went to the baths at LABOURSE. Capt. DRUMMOND continued his lectures. Casualties: 1 O.R. killed & 1 O.R. wounded whilst on working party.	RH
	23.6.16		Companies were attached to Battalions of the 44th Infantry Brigade, for Company training in trenches, as under:- A Company to 7th Batn. Cameron Highlanders B " " 8th " Seaforth " C " " 8/10 " Gordon " D " " 9th " Black Watch Two Lewis Gun teams & 4 Battalion Signallers were attached to each Battalion. Headquarters were transferred to BETHUNE. Casualties: 3 O.R. wounded	JRH

1875 Wt. W593/826 1,000,000 4/15 J.B.C. & A. A.D.S.S./Forms/C. 2118.

13TH (Service) BATTALION.

EAST SURREY REGIMENT. (WANDSWORTH)

120TH INF. BRIGADE.

40TH DIVISION

WAR DIARY
or
INTELLIGENCE SUMMARY

Instructions regarding War Diaries and Intelligence Summaries are contained in F. S. Regs., Part II. and the Staff Manual respectively. Title Pages will be prepared in manuscript.

(Erase heading not required.)

Place	Date	Hour	Summary of Events and Information	Remarks and references to Appendices
BETHUNE	24.6.16		Battalion under instruction in trenches. Casualties 2 O.R. wounded	Nil.
	25.6.16		Ditto. Casualties 1 O.R. killed 11 O.R. wounded	Nil.
	26.6.16		The Battalion left the trenches and concentrated at BETHUNE. A & B Companies were billeted in the Orphanage & C & D Companies on the Graces Factory Casualties 1 O.R. killed	Nil.
	27.6.16		The Battalion received orders to rejoin the 40th Division and marched to BRUAY where billets were found in the North-West part of the town. Headquarters were established at 78.66.	Map Ref. FRANCE Sheet 36A NE Edition 6 20000 Nil.
	28.6.16		Clothes & equipment cleaned. Kit inspections.	Nil.
	29.6.16		The Battalion marched by Companies to the baths.	Nil.
	30.6.16		A & D Companies practised Artillery formation through woods & deploying on reaching open ground from 8.30 – 12.45 Hrs. + exercise with rifles & gas helmets from 14 – 17 Hrs. B & C Companies were versa.	Nil.

W. Newton
Lieut. Colonel,
Commanding 13th (Serv.) Bn. EAST SURREY REGT.

1875 W. W593/826 1,000,000 4/15 J.B.C. & A. A.D.S.S./Forms/C. 2118.

Confidential

War Diary of

13TH (Service) Battalion East Surrey Regt.

FROM 1ST July 1916 TO 31st July 1916

(Volume 2)

Army Form C. 2118

13TH (Service) BATTALION
EAST SURREY REGIMENT (WANDSWORTH) **WAR DIARY**
or
INTELLIGENCE SUMMARY
120TH INF. BRIGADE
40TH DIVISION

(Erase heading not required.)

Instructions regarding War Diaries and Intelligence
Summaries are contained in F. S. Regs., Part II.
and the Staff Manual respectively.   Title Pages
will be prepared in manuscript.

Place	Date	Hour	Summary of Events and Information	Remarks and references to Appendices
BRUAY	1.7.16		The Battalion went for a Route March - MARLES LES MINES - ST.LEONARD - CALONNE RICOUART - CINTRE BRUAY.	Map FRANCE 36 B 3me edition / gr.lt. 1/5
	2.7.16		Brigade Church Parade was held at PLACE DE JULES MARMOTTAN, BRUAY	gr.lt. 2/5
	3.7.16		The Battalion was given instruction in the making of wire entanglements. Orders were received that the 40TH Division was to relieve the 1st Division. holding MAROC & CALONNE Sectors - the 120TH Brigade being in Divisional Reserve.	gr.lt. 3/5 / Map Ref FRANCE
	4.7.16		The Battalion marched to LES BREBIS via BARLIN - HERSIN and relieved the 2nd Battn Munster Fusiliers (3rd Infantry Brigade) Battalion headquarters were established at N°.555 RUE MARÉCHAL FRENCH MINE BUILDINGS, LES BREBIS	Sheet 36NE Edition 6 / 1/20,000 / gr.lt. 4/5
LES BREBIS			do	gr.lt. 5/5
	5.7.16		Parades under Company arrangements.	gr.lt. 5/5
	6.7.16		The Battalion marched by small parties to the Divisional Baths where all spare underclothing was handed in	gr.lt. 6/5
	7.7.16		Parades under Company arrangements	gr.lt. 7/5

1875 Wt. W593/826 1,000,000 4/15 J.B.C. & A. A.D.S.S./Forms/C. 2118.

13TH (Service) BATTALION
EAST SURREY REGIMENT

WAR DIARY
or
INTELLIGENCE SUMMARY
(Erase heading not required.)

Part II. /20TH INF BRIGADE
40TH DIVISION

Instructions regarding War Diaries and Intelligence Summaries are contained in F. S. Regs., Part II. and the Staff Manual respectively. Title Pages will be prepared in manuscript.

Place	Date	Hour	Summary of Events and Information	Remarks and references to Appendices
LES BREBIS	8.7.16		Parades under Company arrangements — wire entanglements & work with gas helmets.	JWHJt.
	9.7.16		Parades under Company arrangements. Casualties. 2/Lieut A Senior & 2 O.R. wounded whilst on a working party. 2/Lt SENIOR reported for duty.	JWHJt.
	10.7.16		Parades under Company arrangements. Orders were received that the Brigade was to relieve the 121st Brigade occupying the MAROC SECTOR.	JWHJt.
MAROC	11.7.16		The Battalion relieved the 12th Battn Suffolk Regt. occupying the right subsection of the MAROC Section. Our front extended from the BANK trench M9d52 to M4c5.6. Battalion Headquarters were established at M9a30 near the junction of TREIZE & NEUF ALLEYS. On our left, the line was held by 11th Battn Kings Own R.L.Rgt. The 14th Battn Argyll & Sutherland Highlanders were in Brigade Support with Headquarters at M3a8.4 and the 14th Battn Highland Light Infantry were in Brigade Reserve with Headquarters at M2 & #89. On our right was the 12th Battn South Wales Borders belonging to the 119th Infantry Brigade.	Map Ref. FRANCE 36c N.W.
				JWHJt.
	12.7.16		Slight shelling by our artillery. Enemy quiet. Casualties 2 O.R. wounded (accidentally)	JWHJt.
	13.7.16		Enemy sent over a few rifle grenades and shells (shrapnel). We retaliated with rifle grenades and our artillery bombarded their front line trenches.	JWHJt.

1875 Wt. W593/826 1,000,000 4/15 J.B.C. & A. A.D.S.S./Forms/C. 2118.

13TH BATTALION
EAST SURREY REGIMENT   120TH INF. BRIGADE
40TH DIVISION

Army Form C. 2118

WAR DIARY
or
INTELLIGENCE SUMMARY
(Erase heading not required.)

Instructions regarding War Diaries and Intelligence
Summaries are contained in F. S. Regs, Part II.
and the Staff Manual respectively.   Title Pages
will be prepared in manuscript.

Place	Date	Hour	Summary of Events and Information	Remarks and references to Appendices
MAROC	13:7:16	etc.	A small party from B Company placed boards in the enemy's wire, giving news of the latest advance of the Allies. Contents roughly as follows: In West – Progress on the SOMME – English have taken 6000 prisoners and the French 9,700, over 80 guns and many machine guns and Minenwerfer. In East. Russians have captured 228,000 Austrians and 2,700 in the district of RIGA also 12,000 Germans near ROVEL.	2R/5/E
	14.7.16		The enemy bombarded the Left of our line with high explosive shells. Our artillery retaliated with considerable effect. The following officers reported for duty 2nd Lieut C.M.JAMES H.S.DAINTREE G.R.ALEXANDER M.W.HAGGER	3R/15/1t.
	15.7.16		The Battalion was relieved by 14th Battalion Highland Light Infantry and became the Brigade Reserve. Accommodation was found in cellars of shell damaged houses near MAROC CHURCH. Headquarters were established about 300 yards N.E of the Church	3R/4/1t.
	16.7.16		Large working parties were supplied for the improvement of trenches in MAROC right subsection. During the night our artillery heavily bombarded the enemy's trenches near LOOS CRATER.	3R/15/1t

1875 W¹. W593/826 1,000,000 4/15 J.B.C. & A. A.D.S.S./Forms/C. 2118.

13TH BATTALION
EAST SURREY REGIMENT

Instructions regarding War Diaries and Intelligence Summaries are contained in F. S. Regs., Part II. and the Staff Manual respectively. Title Pages will be prepared in manuscript.

WAR DIARY

or

INTELLIGENCE SUMMARY

(Erase heading not required.)

/20ᵀᴴ INF. BRIGADE
40ᵀᴴ DIVISION

Army Form C. 2118

Place	Date	Hour	Summary of Events and Information	Remarks and references to Appendices
MAROC	17.7.16	9 P.M.	The Battalion was relieved by the 12ᵗʰ Battⁿ Suffolk Regᵗ & marched by Platoons to LES BREBIS where the former billets were occupied. Casualty. 1 O.R. wounded.	G.R.M.E.
LES BREBIS	18.7.16		Parades under Company arrangements.	G.R.M.E.
	19.7.16		The following officers reported for duty :- Lieut. W.J.CHAMBERS, 2ⁿᵈ Lieut. T.R. THOMSON. D.H.J. MACDONALD - PLAGE, H.FRANKLIN, W.B.HUGHES, C.J.NOAKES, D.E.DODD.	G.R.M.E.
	20.7.16		The Battalion marched by Parties to the Baths.	G.R.M.E.
	21.7.16		All available men were given practice in wearing gas helmets and box respirators. Two parties of 200 men each, went through a cellar in which gas had been liberated. The Signallers and Lewis Gunners took over communications and emplacements respectively from 19ᵗʰ Battⁿ Royal Welsh Fusiliers occupying the right subsection CALONNE Sectr.	G.R.M.E.

1875 Wt. W593/826 1,000,000 4/15 I.B.C. & A. A.D.S.S./Forms/C. 2118.

Army Form C. 2118

WAR DIARY
or
INTELLIGENCE SUMMARY

(Erase heading not required.)

Instructions regarding War Diaries and Intelligence
Summaries are contained in F. S. Regs., Part II.
and the Staff Manual respectively. Title Pages
will be prepared in manuscript.

Place	Date	Hour	Summary of Events and Information	Remarks and references to Appendices
LES BREBIS	22.7.16		The 120th Infantry Brigade relieved the 119th Infantry Brigade occupying the CALONNE Sector. The 13th Battn East Surrey Regt. relieved the 19th Battn Royal Welsh Fusiliers on the right subsection and established Headquarters at M14 d.14 (TEMPLE ST). The left subsection was occupied by the 11th Battn King's Own R.L. Regt. The 14th Battn Argyll + Sutherland	Map Ref 36c 8&1
CALONNE			Highlanders occupied the right subsection MAROC Sector which had been added to the CALONNE Sector. The 14th Battn Highland Light Infantry were in Brigade Support at CALONNE. On our right was the 1st Battn R Marine Light Infantry, belonging to the 188th Brigade, 63rd Royal Naval Division (from the 25th inst.)	R.H.L.t.
	23.7.16		Enemy quiet. Casualties 2/Lt. C.T.NOAKES + 1 O.R. wounded whilst on a wiring party.	R.M.L.t.
	24.7.16		Enemy more active. Several minnenwerfers were dropped near BIRDCAGE WALK and CHAPTEL ALLEY and several whizz bangs on the BURNING BING. We retaliated with French Mortars + 18 pounders.	R.M.L.t.
	25.7.16		Enemy quiet. Few minnenwerfers and whizz bangs during the day. Casualties 6 O.R. wounded.	R.M.L.t.
	26.7.16		Our French Mortars bombarded the CITÉ DE CORNAILLES. Enemy replied with minnenwerfers and whizz bangs. 1 O.R. previously wounded reported for duty.	
			Notification was received that the 63rd R Naval Division, on our right, would be experimenting with poisonous gas during the night, and arrangements were made	

1875 Wt. W593/826 1,000,000 4/15 J.B.C. & A. A.D.S.S./Forms/C. 2118.

13th (Service) BATTALION
EAST SURREY REGIMENT (WANDSWORTH) **WAR DIARY**
or
INTELLIGENCE SUMMARY

(Erase heading not required.)

Army Form C. 2118

Instructions regarding War Diaries and Intelligence Summaries are contained in F. S. Regs., Part II. 120th INF. BRIGADE and the Staff Manual respectively. Title Pages 40th DIVISION will be prepared in manuscript.

Place	Date	Hour	Summary of Events and Information	Remarks and references to Appendices
CALONNE	26.7.16		accordingly for the safety of the Battalion. Later the experiments were postponed.	J.H.H.L.
	27.7.16		Situation normal. Casualties 4 OR wounded. 2/Lt C.J. NOAKES & 1 OR previously wounded reported for duty.	J.H.H.L.
	28.7.16		Enemy sent over several rifle grenades & minenwerfers. One of the latter fell near one of our working parties killing two NCOs and one man. Our French mortars retaliated. Our left Company was relieved by a company of the 14th Battn Highland Light Infantry and became the Reserve Company. The disposition of the Battalion was then two companies in the firing and support lines, one in support and one in reserve. Casualties 3 OR Killed 1 OR wounded.	J.H.H.L.
	29.7.16		Enemy very active with minenwerfers and rifle grenades. We retaliated with 18 pounders and howitzers. The Simallos and Lewis Gunners of the Battalion were relieved by the respective units of the 19th Battn R. Welsh Fusiliers. Casualties 1 OR wounded.	J.H.H.L.
	30.7.16		The Battalion was relieved by the 19th Battn Royal Welsh Fusiliers and marched by platoons into billets at LES BREBIS.	J.H.H.L.

1875   Wt. W593/826   1,000,000   4/15   J.B.C. & A.   A.D.S.S./Forms/C. 2118.

13th (Service) BATTALION

EAST SURREY REGIMENT (WANDSWORTH)

120th INF. BRIGADE

40th DIVISION

Army Form C. 2118

WAR DIARY

or

INTELLIGENCE SUMMARY

(Erase heading not required.)

Instructions regarding War Diaries and Intelligence Summaries are contained in F. S. Regs., Part II. and the Staff Manual respectively. Title Pages will be prepared in manuscript.

Place	Date	Hour	Summary of Events and Information	Remarks and references to Appendices
LES BREBIS	30.7.16		Headquarters were established at L.35.6.2.3 (opposite the Church)	Map Ref 36b N.E. Section 6
			Casualties 30.R. wounded	2000 (R.H.)
	31.7.16		"Battalion resting & cleaning up.	20 N-1/2-

W. Iruston Lieut-Colonel

Condy, 13th (S) Battn East Surrey Regt.

1875   Wt. W593/826   1,000,000   4/15   J.B.C. & A.   A.D.S.S./Forms/C.2118.

WAR DIARY

of

13th. (S) Battn. East Surrey Regt.

From 1st August 1916 to 31st August 1916

Volume 3

Vol 3

13th (Service) BATTALION

EAST SURREY REGIMENT (WANDSWORTH)

WAR DIARY
or
INTELLIGENCE SUMMARY
(Erase heading *not* required.)

/20th INF. BRIGADE.
40th DIVISION

Instructions regarding War Diaries and Intelligence Summaries are contained in F. S. Regs., Part II. and the Staff Manual respectively. Title Pages will be prepared in manuscript.

Place	Date	Hour	Summary of Events and Information	Remarks and references to Appendices
LES BREBIS	1.8.16		Parades under Company arrangements	
	2.8.16		Do	
	3.8.16		The Battalion went by parties to the Divisional Baths whilst on working party. Casualty 1 O.R. wounded	
LOOS	4.8.16		The Battalion relieved the 12th Battn Suffolk Regt. occupying the left subsection LOOS Section. On our right was the 14th Battn. Highland Light Infantry. The 4th Battn Argyll & Sutherland Highlanders was in support. The trenches on our left were held by the 16th Division. Headquarters were established among the ruins of LOOS	
	5.8.16		The enemy sent over about half a dozen Trench Mortar Bombs and blew in a small part of our front line trench. Our trench mortars and Stokes Guns retaliated	
	6.8.16		The enemy presented us with a few rifle grenades, whizz bangs and shrapnel shells. Casualties 2 O.R. wounded	
	7.8.16		The enemy were very active with trench mortars until silenced by our Stokes Guns. Casualties 2 O.R. killed 5 O.R. wounded.	

1875 Wt. W593/826 1,000,000 4/15 J.B.C. & A. A.D.S.S./Forms/C. 2118.

Army Form C. 2118

WAR DIARY

or

INTELLIGENCE SUMMARY

(*Erase heading not required.*)

1/3ª (Service) BATTALION
EAST SURREY REGIMENT

Instructions regarding War Diaries and Intelligence
Summaries are contained in F. S. Regs, Part II.
and the Staff Manual respectively. Title Pages / 120ᵗʰ INF. BRIGADE,
will be prepared in manuscript. 40ᵀᴴ DIVISION

Place	Date	Hour	Summary of Events and Information	Remarks and references to Appendices
LOOS	8.8.16		We bombarded the enemys lines with rifle grenades, Stokes guns and trench mortars in order to test the relative strengths of the enemy and ourselves with regard to these weapons. The enemy retaliated but we completely subdued their fire without the aid of our artillery. Casualties 5 O.R. killed and 10 O.R. wounded	K.H.L.
	9.8.16		The 120ᵗʰ Brigade were relieved by a Brigade of the 16ᵗʰ Division. The Battalion were relieved as under — Headquarters and 2 Companies by 9ᵗʰ Battⁿ Leinster Regt. 1 Company 8ᵗʰ Battⁿ Inniskillen Fusiliers 1 Company 6ᵗʰ Battⁿ Connaught Rangers.	
N. MAROC			The Battalion moved into billets occupied by the 12ᵗʰ Battⁿ Suffolk Regt. at N. MAROC and became the Brigade Reserve. Headquarters were established about 300 yards N.E. of MAROC CHURCH. The billets consisted of cellars of damaged houses. Casualties 20R wounded	K.H.L.
	10.8.16		Small working & fatigue parties provided. Remainder resting.	K.H.L.
	11.8.16		Dº Dº	K.H.L.

1875 Wt. W593/826 1,000,000 4/15 J.B.C. & A. A.D.S.S./Forms/C. 2118.

Army Form C. 2118

13TH (Service) BATTALION
EAST SURREY REGIMENT   WAR DIARY
or
INTELLIGENCE SUMMARY
(Erase heading not required.)

1/20TH INF. BRIGADE
40TH DIVISION

Instructions regarding War Diaries and Intelligence
Summaries are contained in F. S. Regs., Part II.
and the Staff Manual respectively. Title Pages
will be prepared in manuscript.

Place	Date	Hour	Summary of Events and Information	Remarks and references to Appendices
N.MAROC	12.8.16		The Battalion were relieved by the 20th Battn. Middlesex Regt. and marched into billets vacated by them at PETIT SAIN. Headquarters were established at No 209 RUE DE MAZINGARBE.	R.W.M.
PETIT SAIN	13.8.16		The Battalion marched by parties to the Divisional Baths at LES BREBIS. Casualties 2 O.R. wounded whilst on working party	R.W.M.
	14.8.16		Church Parade in a field W. of the RUE DE LA MAIRIE.	R.W.M.
	15.8.16		Orders were received that the 120th Inf. Brigade was to relieve the 119th Inf. Brigade occupying the CALONNE Sector.	R.W.M.
CALONNE	16.8.16		The Battalion relieved the 19th Battn. Royal Welch Fusiliers holding the right subsection, CALONNE Sector. During the afternoon the enemy shelled BIRDCAGE WALK and the firing line at M.20 B.3.4.5. Our French mortars silenced them	Map Ref. 36.e. 1. S.1. R.W.M.
	17.8.16		The enemy sent over many rifle grenades and trench mortar bombs in the centre of our front and support lines. also several minnjens + aerial darts on the left of our line. Our stokes guns + trench mortars retaliated. Casualties 1 O.R. killed 1 O.R. wounded.	R.W.M.

1875 Wt. W593/826 1,000,000 4/15 J.B.C. & A. A.D.S.S./Forms/C. 2118.

13TH (Service) BATTALION
EAST SURREY REGIMENT

WAR DIARY
or
INTELLIGENCE SUMMARY
(Erase heading not required.)

Instructions regarding War Diaries and Intelligence
Summaries are contained in F. S. Regs. Part II. /20TH INF. BRIGADE
and the Staff Manual respectively. Title Pages   HOM DIVISION
will be prepared in manuscript.

Place	Date	Hour	Summary of Events and Information	Remarks and references to Appendices
CALONNE	18.8.16		Between 4 p.m. to 6 p.m. we bombarded the enemy's front line with rifle grenades + our Stokes guns, trench mortars + artillery bombarded CITÉ DE CORNAILLE, causing considerable damage. The enemy retaliated with 77 m.m. rifle grenades, aerial darts and a few rum jars, but with little effect. Casualties : Lieut. W.J. CHAMBERS + 1 OR. killed ; Capt. M.J. PEMBERTON + 3 OR. wounded.	R.Hg.L.
	19.8.16		During the day the enemy were active with 77 m.m. + aerial darts. Our artillery shelled the Reserve line behind CITÉ DE CORNAILLE. A Divisional test Gas Alarm was held at 4 p.m. The gas arrangements were reported satisfactory. Casualties : 2 OR. killed. 4 OR. wounded.	R.Hg.L.
	20.8.16		The Battalion was relieved by the 14th Battn. Highland Light Infantry + moved into billets at CALONNE. Headquarters were established at M.14.d 1.2.¾. (100 yds NNW + COVENT GARDEN) Between 10.30 p.m. + 12 midnight our artillery kept up a very heavy bombardment of the enemy's lines whilst the 63rd Royal Naval Division holding the line on the right of CALONNE set free a quantity of poisonous gas. Casualties : Capt. L.R. MERRYFIELD, 2/L. G.R.FIELDING + 1 OR. wounded.	See Rept. 36 G.SW.1 R.Hg.L.

1875 Wt. W593/826 1,000,000 4/15 I.B.C. & A. A.D.S.S./Forms/C. 2118.

WAR DIARY

or

INTELLIGENCE SUMMARY

(Erase heading not required.)

13TH (Service) BATTALION
EAST SURREY REGIMENT

Instructions regarding War Diaries and Intelligence
Summaries are contained in F. S. Regs., Part II. 120TH INF. BRIGADE
and the Staff Manual respectively. Title Pages 40TH DIVISION
will be prepared in manuscript.

Place	Date	Hour	Summary of Events and Information	Remarks and references to Appendices
CALONNE.	21.8.16		The Battalion was employed on working and carrying parties. Situation quiet.	AdM.L.
	22.8.16		During the day our artillery were engaged cutting the wire around M 21 a 05.70 and registering for a barrage around that spot. At 9.30 p.m. a raiding party from the 14th Bn. Highland Light Infantry crossed Noman's Land & entered the enemy's trenches. They encountered a German working party, causing several casualties & returned with a wounded prisoner. During this time our 18pounders & trawtzers together with Stokes guns trench mortars kept up a heavy bombardment.	36 c.s.w.1
	23.8.16		All available men were used for working parties. At 11 p.m. a party from the 14th Argyll & Sutherland Hrs. raided the enemy's trenches about M 15 d 40.83 but met none of the enemy.	AdM.L.
	24.8.16		The Battalion relieved the 14th Bn. Highland Light Left Relieving Right Lubeckton CALONNE. On our left were the 11th Bn. King's Own R.L. Rgt. on our right were the 63rd R. Naval Div.	AdM.L.
	25.8.16		At 5 a.m. our trench mortars bombarded the enemy's support lines. The Huns did not retaliate. During the afternoon however, they sent over a shower of aerial darts. Casualties:- 2 OR. killed. 5 OR wounded.	AdM.L.

1875 Wt. W 593/826 1,000,000 4/15 J.B.C. & A. A.D.S.S./Forms/C. 2118.

WAR DIARY

or

INTELLIGENCE SUMMARY

(Erase heading not required.)

13th (Service) BATTALION
EAST SURREY REGIMENT
20th INF. BRIGADE
40th DIVISION

Instructions regarding War Diaries and Intelligence Summaries are contained in F. S. Regs., Part II. and the Staff Manual respectively. Title Pages will be prepared in manuscript.

Place	Date	Hour	Summary of Events and Information	Remarks and references to Appendices
CALONNE	26.8.16		During the afternoon the enemy were very active with aerial darts and trench mortars. Our artillery & trench mortars retaliated with considerable effect. About 10 p.m. the heavy guns around LES BREBIS & HAZINGARBE commenced to bombard the enemy's lines away on our left. They kept up a severe bombardment for about an hour. Casualties 1 O.R. killed, 2 O.R. wounded.	
	27.8.16		Enemy very quiet except for occasional aerial darts. Casualties: 2nd Lieut. H FRANKLIN + 1 O.R. wounded	
	28.8.16		Our trench mortars sent a number of bombs into CITÉ DE CORNAILLE but the enemy did not retaliate. During the night we placed on the enemy's wire, and sent into the enemy's trenches by means of rifle grenades, notices in German, stating that RUMANIA had declared war against GERMANY and AUSTRIA. Casualties - Nil.	
	29.8.16		Situation quiet. During the afternoon our medium trench mortars sent several bombs into CITÉ DE CORNAILLE. The enemy did not retaliate. Casualties - Nil	

1875 Wt. W593/826 1,000,000 4/15 J.B.C. & A. A.D.S.S./Forms/C. 2118.

13TH (SERVICE) BATTALION

EAST SURREY REGIMENT

Instructions regarding War Diaries and Intelligence
Summaries are contained in F. S. Regs., Part II.
and the Staff Manual respectively. Title Pages 120TH INF. BRIGADE
will be prepared in manuscript.

40TH DIVISION

WAR DIARY

or

INTELLIGENCE SUMMARY

(Erase heading not required.)

Place	Date	Hour	Summary of Events and Information	Remarks and references to Appendices
CALONNE	30.8.16		The Battalion was relieved by the 1st Battalion Honourable Artillery Company of the 190th Brigade 63rd R. Naval Division & marched to LES BREBIS where it occupied billets in Area D. Battalion Headquarters were established at No. 525 bis, Rue de MARÉCHAL FRENCH. Casualties Nil.	LES BREBIS
LES BREBIS	31.8.16		The Battalion was resting & cleaning up. Kit & rifle inspections were held under Company arrangements.	

W. Winton Lieut-Col
Comdg. 13th (S) Battr. East Surrey Regt.

1875 W. W.593/826 1,000,000 4/15 J.B.C. &A. A.D.S.S./Forms/C. 2118

Vol 4

H.O
Exhibit

WAR DIARY

OF

13TH BN EAST SURREY REGT.

VOLUME 4.

1ST SEPTEMBER to 30TH SEPTEMBER 1916

Army Form C. 2118

WAR DIARY
or
INTELLIGENCE SUMMARY
(Erase heading not required.)

13ᵗʰ BATTALION
EAST SURREY REGIMENT

Instructions regarding War Diaries and Intelligence Summaries are contained in F. S. Regs., Part II. and the Staff Manual respectively. Title Pages will be prepared in manuscript.

20ᵗʰ INF BDE
40ᵗʰ DIVISION

Place	Date	Hour	Summary of Events and Information	Remarks and references to Appendices
LES BREBIS	1.9.16		The Battalion went to the Baths by small parties. It was reported that CAPT. L.R. MERRYFIELD who was wounded on the 18ᵗʰ ultimo had died of wounds on the 28ᵗʰ. 2ⁿᵈ Lieut A.C. THOMPSON reported himself for duty.	
	2.9.16		Parades under Company arrangements. Casualties:- 6 O.R. wounded (4 by bomb accident. 1 by bullet fired at an aeroplane + 1 shock). The Commanding Officer Lieut Col W.C. NEWTON was evacuated to Corps Rest Station suffering from trench fever. 2ⁿᵈ Lieut. E.E. DODD was also evacuated to Corps Rest Stn. (sick)	
	3.9.16		Church Parades were held by the Padre (Capt. SPINNEY) in the Church Army Hut. Half the Battalion at 9 a.m. the other half at 11 a.m.	
	4.9.16		Parades under Company arrangements.	
S. MAROC	5.9.16		The Battalion relieved the 12ᵗʰ Battⁿ Suffolk Regt. in Brigade Reserve at S. MAROC. Headquarters were established at M 2 d 1.4.	

1875 Wt. W⁵593/826 1,000,000 4/15 J.B.C. & A. A.D.S.S./Forms/C. 2118.

WAR DIARY

or

INTELLIGENCE SUMMARY

(Erase heading not required.)

13TH BATTALION
EAST SURREY REGIMENT

Instructions regarding War Diaries and Intelligence
Summaries are contained in F. S. Regs., Part II.
and the Staff Manual respectively. Title Pages
will be prepared in manuscript.

/20TH INF BRIGADE
40TH DIVISION

Place	Date	Hour	Summary of Events and Information	Remarks and references to Appendices
S. MAROC	6.9.16		Large working Parties provided for the R. Engineers employed on improvement of billets — cellars cleared, whitewashed + strengthened beds (three tier) erected in several cellars. Situation quiet.	
	7.9.16		Work on billets continued with a view to the coming winter. During the day the neighbouring artillery were active cutting the enemy's wire S of the DOUBLE CRASSIER.	
	8.9.16		All available men employed on whitewashing + laying sandbags on cellar roofs. Situation quiet.	
	9.9.16		Improvement of billets continued. Situation quiet.	
	10.9.16		Large working + carrying Parties for R.E. Enemy sent a number of shrapnel shells just beyond our billets.	
	11.9.16		Work on billets continued. Situation quiet. Casualties 1 O.R. killed	

1875 Wt. W593/826 1,000,000 4/15 J.B.C. & A. A.D.S.S./Forms/C. 2118.

WAR DIARY
or
INTELLIGENCE SUMMARY

(Erase heading not required.)

13TH BATTALION
EAST SURREY REGIMENT
120th INF. BDE
40th DIVISION.

Instructions regarding War Diaries and Intelligence
Summaries are contained in F.S. Regs., Part II.
and the Staff Manual respectively. Title Pages
will be prepared in manuscript.

Place	Date	Hour	Summary of Events and Information	Remarks and references to Appendices
MAROC	12.9.16		The Battalion relieved the 14th Bn. Highland Light Infantry holding the right subsection MAROC Sector. Headquarters were established at M.3.c.20.05. On our right was the 63rd R. Naval Division. on our left 11 Bn. Kings Own R.L.R. Our medium trench mortars were active cutting wire in front of PUITS 16 bombarding the enemy's lines South of the DOUBLE CRASSIER. The enemy retaliated with rifle grenades. In the afternoon the enemy shelled our support line between EDGWARE ROAD & NEUF ALLEY with 5.9"s	[initials]
	13.9.16		Our medium trench mortars were active wire cutting in front of PUITS 16. The enemy retaliated with minimal shells into EDGWARE KEEP and about 30 shells (shrapnel) into our support line near M9 & M9. They also fired several rifle grenades at BANK SAP but these fell short.	[initials]
	14.9.16		Wire cutting in front of PUITS 16 was continued. The enemy retaliated with about 12 minimal shells to high explosive (5.9") into EDGWARE KEEP. During the night the Lewis Guns traversed the enemy's wire.	[initials]
	15.9.16		The enemy shelled our front and support trenches between EDGWARE RD and the DOUBLE CRASSIER with 5.9", shrapnel trench mortars. A raid on the enemy trenches was contemplated but abandoned. Casualties 1 O.R. wounded (died of wounds at C.C.S.)	[initials]

1875 Wt. W593/826 1,000,000 4/15 J.B.C. & A. A.D.S.S./Forms/C. 2118.

WAR DIARY

or

INTELLIGENCE SUMMARY

(Erase heading not required.)

13ᵗʰ BATTALION
EAST SURREY REGIMENT.

Instructions regarding War Diaries and Intelligence
Summaries are contained in F. S. Regs., Part II.
and the Staff Manual respectively. Title Pages
will be prepared in manuscript.

Title Pages 120ᵗʰ INF. BDE
40ᵗʰ DIV.

Place	Date	Hour	Summary of Events and Information	Remarks and references to Appendices
MA ROC	16.9.16		During the day the enemy dropped shells along our support line causing no damage.	
		11.30 p.m.	At 11.30 p.m. we attempted a raid on the enemys trenches but were unable to penetrate the enemys wire. 2nd Lieut F.C. JOHNSTON & 2nd Lieut G.S. DREW reported for duty. Casualties :- 2nd Lieut THOMSON (T.R.) & 3 o.r wounded ; 1 o.r missing and 2 o.r missing, believed wounded.	[initials] Lt.
	17.9.16		Artillery fairly active on both sides. The enemy sent a number of Minenwerfers and aerial torpedoes near NEUF KEEP but did no damage.	[initials] Lt.
	18.9.16		The enemy sent several Minenwerfers in to our support and reserve trenches causing damage in several places. 2nd Lieuts. G.B. BISSET & C.E.S. COOPER reported for duty.	[initials] Lt.
	19.9.16		Our artillery shelled the enemys trenches South of the DOUBLE CRASSIER. The enemy retaliated with several Minenwerfers on to our Reserve line. We were relieved by the 14ᵗʰ Bn. Welch Regt (119ᵗʰ Inf. Brigade) & marched into billets at LES BREBIS. Headquarters were established opposite the Church. 2nd Lieut W.H. MORRIS reported for duty.	[initials] Lt.

1875 Wt. W593/826 1,009,000 4/15 J.B.C. & A. A.D.S.S./Forms/C. 2118.

WAR DIARY

or

INTELLIGENCE SUMMARY

(Erase heading not required.)

13TH BATTALION
EAST SURREY REGIMENT

Instructions regarding War Diaries and Intelligence
Summaries are contained in F. S. Regs., Part II,
and the Staff Manual respectively. Title Pages
will be prepared in manuscript.

Part II. /20th INF. BDE
40TH DIVISION

Place	Date	Hour	Summary of Events and Information	Remarks and references to Appendices
LES BREBIS	20.9.16		The Battalion were resting & cleaning up. A Company attended a Flammenwerfer demonstration.	AN/Lr
	21.9.16		The Commanding Officer, Company Commanders & specialist officers reconnoitred the Brigade Support positions in 14 Bis (LOOS) Sector.	AN/Lr
LOOS	22.9.16		The 120th Infantry Brigade relieved the 96th Inf. Brigade in the 14 Bis Sector.	AN/Lr
PUITS 14 Bis Sector			The 13th Bn. East Surrey Regt. relieved the 1st Bn. Gordon Highlanders in Brigade Support. Headquarters were established near the junction of SOUTHERN SAP & TENTH AVENUE. The trenches dug outs in this Sector were in a very bad condition.	AN/Lr
	23.9.16		All available men employed cleaning & improving trenches & dug outs. Situation quiet	AN/Lr
	24.9.16		Work on trenches continued. Large working parties supplied to the R.E.	AN/Lr
	25.9.16		Situation quiet. A gas alarm was given by a Brigade on our right but no traces of gas reached us. Lt.Col. W.C. NEWTON & 2nd Lieut E.E. DODD returned from Corps Rest Station	AN/Lr

1875 Wt. W593/826 1,000,000 4/15 J.B.C. & A. A.D.S.S./Forms/C.2118.

WAR DIARY

or

INTELLIGENCE SUMMARY

(Erase heading not required.)

13TH BATTALION
EAST SURREY REGIMENT

Instructions regarding War Diaries and Intelligence
Summaries are contained in F. S. Regs., Part II.
and the Staff Manual respectively. Title Pages
will be prepared in manuscript.

120 TH INF. BRIGADE
40TH DIVISION

Place	Date	Hour	Summary of Events and Information	Remarks and references to Appendices
14 bis	26.9.16		The Battalion relieved the 14th Bn. Argyll Sutherland Highlanders in the left sub section 14 bis. Headquarters were established in RESERVE TRENCH at 6.30 & 3.5. On our right was the 11th Bn Kings Own Regt. on our left. The 8th Division. Casualties 1 or wounded.	✓
	27.9.16		Our trench mortars fired several rounds into Buis 14 bis. The enemy retaliated on POSEN ALLEY.	✓
	28.9.16		The enemy trench mortars fired a number of rounds in to POSEN ALLEY and MEATH TRENCH. Our medium trench mortars were active were cutting opposite 14 bis.	✓
	29.9.16		Our stokes guns trench mortars bombarded the enemy's lines between 5 pm to 6 pm. During the night we attempted a small raid on the enemy's trenches opposite Boyau 63. The bangalore torpedo did not cut the wire sufficiently & the party were unable to get through.	✓
	30.9.16		The Battalion was relieved by the 14th Bn Argyll Sutherland Highlanders & marched into billets in MAZINGARBE.	✓

W. Newton Lt. Col.
Comdg. 13th (K) Battn. East Surrey Regt.

1875 Wt. W593/826 1,000,000 4/15 J.B.C. & A. A.D.S.S./Forms/C. 2118.

Vol 5

5. D
12 sheets

WAR DIARY

OF

13TH BN EAST SURREY REGT.

VOLUME 5

1ST OCTOBER TO 31ST OCTOBER 1916

Army Form C. 2118

13ᵗʰ (Service) BATTALION
EAST SURREY REGIMENT
/20ᵗʰ INF. BRIGADE
40ᵗʰ DIVISION

WAR DIARY
or
INTELLIGENCE SUMMARY
(Erase heading not required.)

Instructions regarding War Diaries and Intelligence
Summaries are contained in F.S. Regs., Part II.
and the Staff Manual respectively. Title Pages
will be prepared in manuscript.

Place	Date	Hour	Summary of Events and Information	Remarks and references to Appendices
MAZINGARBE	1.10.16		The Battalion occupied the Southern Huts in MAZINGARBE. Report on attempted raid by Party under Lieut. E.B. BUCKLAND is given in APPENDIX I.	QRIKyL
	2.10.16		The Battalion now resting and cleaning up. The Baths at the Brewery were allotted to the Battalion — no change of underclothing was, however, available.	GRHyL
	3.10.16		Thorough rifle, kit and equipment inspections were held.	GRHyL
14 bro	4.10.16		The Battalion relieved the 14ᵗʰ Battalion Argyll & Sutherland Highlanders in the left subsection, 14 bro Sector. Headquarters were established at G.30.d. 35 near the junction of RESERVE TRENCH and HUGO LANE. During the night three bursts of rapid fire, each of three minutes duration were fired from every rifle and Lewis Gun in the front line. Our Trench Mortars opened a five minutes heavy bombardment at 8.4 pm. and another at 10.34 pm. A patrol went out under Lieut. T.F. DAVIS and was reported missing. Casualties: Lieut. E.B. BUCKLAND killed.	MRHyL

1875 Wt. W593/826 1,000,000 4/15 J.B.C. & A. A.D.S.S./Forms/C. 2118.

WAR DIARY
or
INTELLIGENCE SUMMARY

(Erase heading not required.)

13ᵗʰ (Service) BATTALION
EAST SURREY REGIMENT
/20ᵗʰ INF. BRIGADE
40ᵗʰ DIVISION

Instructions regarding War Diaries and Intelligence
Summaries are contained in F. S. Regs., Part II.
and the Staff Manual respectively. Title Pages
will be prepared in manuscript.

Place	Date	Hour	Summary of Events and Information	Remarks and references to Appendices
14 bis	5.10.16		In cooperation with the 8ᵗʰ Division on our left, three gas and three smoke attacks were launched against the enemy. At specified times our Trench Mortars, machine guns, Lewis guns and rifles opened rapid fire on the enemy front line, support line and communication trenches.	
			Report on patrol under Lieut DAVIS is given in APPENDIX II	
			Report on Minor operations is given in APPENDIX III	
			Casualties :- 1 o.r. killed ; Lieut T.F. DAVIS and 3 o.r. wounded ; 1 o.r. slightly gassed.	JRH/L
	6.10.16		Situation very quiet.	JRH/L
	7.10.16		The enemy sent a few French mortar bombs into ROSEN ALLEY and MEATH TRENCH. Our Stokes guns retaliate.	
			Casualties :- 1 o.r. killed.	JRH/L
	8.10.16		The Battalion was relieved by the 14ᵗʰ Battn Argyll & Sutherland Highlanders and moves into Brigade Support. Headquarters were established near the junction of TENTH AVENUE and SOUTHERN SAP.	JRH/L
	9.10.16		Situation quiet. Large working parties provided for the R.E.	JRH/L

1875 Wt. W593/826 1,000,000 4/15. J.B.C. & A. A.D.S.S./Forms/C. 2118.

WAR DIARY
or
INTELLIGENCE SUMMARY

(Erase heading not required.)

13th (Service) BATTALION
EAST SURREY REGIMENT

120th INF BRIGADE
40th DIVISION

Instructions regarding War Diaries and Intelligence
Summaries are contained in F. S. Regs., Part II.
and the Staff Manual respectively. Title Pages
will be prepared in manuscript.

Place	Date	Hour	Summary of Events and Information	Remarks and references to Appendices
14 his	10.10.16		Situation quiet. Large working parties provided for R.E.	2Lt...
	11.10.16		All available men on working fatigue parties.	2Lt...
	12.10.16		The Battalion was relieved by the 13th Battn. Yorks. Regt. (121st Inf Bde) and moved via TENTH AVENUE to the left subsection HULLUCH sector. The subsection extended from VENDIN ALLEY to Bruay 77 and WINGS WAY. Headquarters were established in MULLINS WAY near the junction of NINTH AVENUE and HAY ALLEY. On our left was the 12th Battn. Northumberland Fusiliers. On our right the 11th Kings R.L. Regt.	2Lt...
HULLUCH	13.10.16		Situation active. Throughout the day the enemy threw Rum jars & minenwerfer into our front and support lines behind the HULLUCH CRATERS. Our howitzers (4.2). 18 pdrs. stokes guns and trench mortars retaliated with considerable effect. Casualties: 1 or killed; 1 or died of wounds; 2 or wounded.	2Lt...
	14.10.16		Situation active. Enemy continued to throw rum jars and minenwerfer into GREEN CURVE. Our stokes guns and artillery retaliated. Casualties 1 or killed 2 or wounded)	2Lt...
	15.10.16		At intervals throughout the day the enemy threw rum jars + minenwerfer into our trenches behind HULLUCH CRATERS. Slight artillery retaliation. Casualties: 6 OR wounded	2Lt...

1875   Wt. W593/826   1,000,000   4/15   J.B.C. & A.   A.D.S.S./Forms/C.2118.

Army Form C. 2118

WAR DIARY
or
~~INTELLIGENCE SUMMARY~~
(Erase heading not required.)

13TH BATTALION
EAST SURREY REGIMENT
120TH INF BRIGADE
40TH DIVISION

Instructions regarding War Diaries and Intelligence Summaries are contained in F.S. Regs., Part II. and the Staff Manual respectively. Title Pages will be prepared in manuscript.

Place	Date	Hour	Summary of Events and Information	Remarks and references to Appendices
HULLUCH	16.10.16		The enemy sent large numbers of aerial darts and a few rum jars into our front and support lines. Casualties 3 or wounded.	
	17.10.16		Our artillery sent a number of shells into the enemy's front support lines opposite the HULLUCH CRATERS. Enemy fairly quiet. Casualties 1 or killed, 2 or wounded.	
PHILOSOPHE.	18.10.16		The Battalion was relieved by the 14th Battn Argyll & Sutherland Highlanders and marched into Brigade Reserve billets at PHILOSOPHE (W). Casualties 4 or wounded.	
	19.10.16		The Battalion bathes at MAZINGARBE BREWERY.	
	20.10.16		Parades under company arrangements. Large working parties supplied to R.E.	
	21.10.16		Do.	
	22.10.16		Do. Major E.B. POOLE was attached for instruction.	
	23.10.16		The Battalion bathes at MAZINGARBE. Divisional schools closed. Major F.C.B. JOHNSON took over command 17th Pl Watch Post (119th Pde)	

1875 W₁ W593/826 1,009,000 4/15 J.B.C. & A. A.D.S.S./Forms/C. 2118.

WAR DIARY

or

INTELLIGENCE SUMMARY.

(Erase heading not required.)

13TH BATTALION
EAST SURREY REGIMENT.

Instructions regarding War Diaries and Intelligence
Summaries are contained in F. S. Regs., Part II.
and the Staff Manual respectively. Title pages
will be prepared in manuscript.

120TH INF. BRIGADE
40TH DIVISION

Place	Date	Hour	Summary of Events and Information	Remarks and references to Appendices
PHILOSOPHE	24.10.16		Large carrying parties were found for the removal of empty gas cylinders from HULLUCH sector. Small Box Respirators were issued to the Battalion	W.N.J.
	25.10.16		The Battalion was relieved by the 1st Battalion Staffordshire Regiment (24th Division) and marched to billets at PETIT SAINS. Headquarters were established at 209, Rue de Masingarbe.	W.N.J.
PETIT SAINS	26.10.16		Parades under Company arrangements.	W.N.J.
BRUAY	27.10.16		The Battalion marched to BRUAY. Headquarters were established at in RUE DE LA MAIR 15.	W.N.J. A.N.J.
MAGNICOURT EN-COMTÉ.	28.10.16		The Battalion marched into billets at MAGNICOURT-EN-COMTÉ. Headquarters were established at the Ecole (Garçons). Brigade Headquarters were at LA THIEULOYE.	W.N.J.
AVERDOINGT	29.10.16		The Battalion marched via BAILLEUL-AUX-CORNAILLES to AVERDOINGT. Headquarters were established at the Ecole & the Brigade Hqrs. were at FOUFFIN-RICAMETZ. Lieut T.F.DAVIS rejoined.	W.N.J. W.N.J.
	30.10.16		Parades under Company arrangements.	W.N.J.
	31.10.16		The Battalion carried out a Programme of Training in Physical Drill, Arms Drill, Box respirator drill & musketry.	W.N.J.

W. Newton
Lieut-Colonel
Cmdg 13th Battn. East Surrey Regt.

2353 Wt. W2544/1454 700,000 5/15 D. D. & L.   A.D.S.S./Forms/C 2118.

Army Form C. 2118

13TH BATTALION
EAST SURREY REGIMENT.
120TH INF. BRIGADE
40TH DIVISION.

WAR DIARY
or
INTELLIGENCE SUMMARY

(Erase heading not required.)

Instructions regarding War Diaries and Intelligence
Summaries are contained in F. S. Regs, Part II.
and the Staff Manual respectively. Title Pages
will be prepared in manuscript.

Place	Date	Hour	Summary of Events and Information	Remarks and references to Appendices

APPENDIX I.

Report on Minor Operation carried out by the 13th Bn. East Surrey Regt on the night of the 29/30th September 1916.

1. The party responsible for laying of line from Boyau 63 to enemy's sap front left at time appointed & experienced no difficulty in executing the duty allotted to them.

2. The Bangalore Party left Boyau 63 at 10 p.m. and arrived with the torpedo at the mouth of the enemy's sap without being discovered by the enemy. This party experienced some difficulty in getting the torpedo into position. Lieut F.N. CORBEN returned to Boyau 63 and reported the matter to Capt L.B. MILLS. The Corporal of the R.E. then proceeded to the sap head and succeeded after taking one section out of the torpedo, in placing it in position. He then returned to Boyau 63.

3. The Raiding and Covering Parties left Boyau 63 at the time appointed

4. The Artillery appeared to be a couple of minutes late in opening fire. The torpedo was sprung immediately the bombardment commenced.

1875 Wt. W593/826 1,000,000 4/15 J.B.C. & A. A.D.S.S./Forms/C. 2118.

・ 13th BATTALION
EAST SURREY REGT.
120th INF. BRIGADE
40th DIVISION.

WAR DIARY
or
INTELLIGENCE SUMMARY

(Erase heading not required.)

Instructions regarding War Diaries and Intelligence Summaries are contained in F. S. Regs., Part II. and the Staff Manual respectively. Title Pages will be prepared in manuscript.

Place	Date	Hour	Summary of Events and Information	Remarks and references to Appendices
			Sheet 2. APPENDIX I.	
			5. Immediately the torpedo was sprung the Raiding Party rushed forward and entered the enemy's Sap. They found that the torpedo had done its work with great efficiency. The covertina wire which had previously filled the Sap and the wire which had stretched across the top of it had disappeared and the way was clear. On proceeding down the Sap it was found that a corner existed in it and that from this corner to the enemy's fire trench the Sap was filled with a second lot of wire both in and over it and that their further progress was barred. The Party spent 40 minutes or about the Sap endeavouring to find a gap through which to enter the enemy's lines but were unsuccessful.	
			6. The whole operation was carried through without any hitch whatever and the excellence of the second line of wire was in my opinion the only bar to bringing the raid to a successful issue. It appears to have been a complete surprise and our movements were unhindered by hostile fire. No casualties were sustained during the operations nor did the enemy retaliate on my line afterwards.	

1875 Wt. W593/826 1,000,000 4/15 J.B.C. & A. A.D.S.S./Forms/C. 2118.

Army Form C. 2118

13ᵗʰ BATTALION
EAST SURREY REGT.

Instructions regarding War Diaries and Intelligence Summaries are contained in F. S. Regs., Part II. and the Staff Manual respectively. Title Pages will be prepared in manuscript.

WAR DIARY
or
INTELLIGENCE SUMMARY
(*Erase heading not required.*)

Place	Date	Hour	Summary of Events and Information	Remarks and references to Appendices
			Sheet 3 APPENDIX I	
			I. I consider that the R.E. Corporal (Cpl BAMBER) did his work in a very efficient and praiseworthy manner which I wish to bring to your notice.	
			1/10/16.	
			(signd) W. Newton Lieut Col.	
			Commanding 13ᵗʰ Bn. East Surrey Regiment.	

1875 Wt. W593/826 1,000,000 4/15 J.B.C. & A. A.D.S.S./Forms/C. 2118.

WAR DIARY
or
INTELLIGENCE SUMMARY

(Erase heading not required.)

Instructions regarding War Diaries and Intelligence Summaries are contained in F. S. Regs., Part II. and the Staff Manual respectively. Title Pages will be prepared in manuscript.

Place	Date	Hour	Summary of Events and Information	Remarks and references to Appendices

APPENDIX II

T.L. 120th Infantry Brigade.

I beg to report that the Patrol under LIEUT. DAVIS which left my lines on the night of the 4/5th October and was reported by me on the morning of the 5th as MISSING has since returned. Lieut. Davis is slightly wounded; one O.R. killed, two O.R. slightly wounded.

Two Patrols consisting of one officer and 3 O.R. left Argau 54 on the night of the 4/5th October at 12.30 a.m. and proceeded to the enemy's lines at H35. d.2. 2 for the purpose of keeping the enemy wire which had been cut by our T.M's under observation and to report its being repaired; also if possible, to capture a prisoner or bring back any intelligence.

On reaching the gap in the wire Lieut. Davis discovered that some coils of the concertina wire had been placed close to the gap, —————— He anticipated that two half teams replaced for the purpose of repairing the gap, so waited on the chance of capturing a prisoner from a working party. The teams no sign of life in the enemy's trenches, and as daylight was approaching he decided to withdraw.

On reaching the neighbourhood of our wire a Machine Gun opened fire, and inflicted the casualties mentioned. Lieut. Davis being uncertain of his whereabouts, withdrew the party into a neighbouring Shell-hole and awaited daylight. They remained there without food or water until 7 P.m. (when it was dark enough to return to our lines.

The man killed has been located to-day and will be brought in during the night.

I consider the conduct of Lieut. Davis, under very trying circumstances, is very praiseworthy, for the coolness and resource shown by him on a sudden emergency. He states that his men behaved excellently under the very trying circumstances in which they were placed.

6/10/16

(Signed) W. Newton Lieut. Col.
Commanding 13th Bn. East Surrey Regt.

1875 Wt. W593/826 1,000,000 4/15 J.B.C. & A. A.D.S.S./Forms/C.2118.

13TH BATTALION
EAST SURREY REGT.
120TH INFANTRY BRIGADE
40TH DIVISION

Army Form C. 2118

WAR DIARY
or
INTELLIGENCE SUMMARY
(Erase heading not required.)

Instructions regarding War Diaries and Intelligence
Summaries are contained in F. S. Regs, Part II.
and the Staff Manual respectively. Title Pages
will be prepared in manuscript.

Place	Date	Hour	Summary of Events and Information	Remarks and references to Appendices

APPENDIX III

H.Q. 130TH INFANTRY BRIGADE.

MINOR OPERATION. Night 5th/6th Oct. 1916

The operation carried out on the night of the 5th/6th Oct. '16, as far as the LEFT BN. 14½ BIS
SECTOR was concerned, passed off without a hitch.

The Programme and Time Table was carried through in the entirety.

On my left front the Tunnelers which contained "RATS" were concealed with the
exception of Lewis Gunners and Orderlies at the time laid down, altho' "ZEPPELIN YORK" had
not then been received by me. It was reported to me that the Lewis Gunners on this sector did
specially good work. At the other two Company fronts, the Smoke Attacks were launched at the
appointed time, and worked well.

The enemy's retaliation was weak, and consisted of a few number of Aerial Darts and
Rifle Grenades, fired on the front and Support lines, causing little or no damage. About 20 rounds
of Shrapnel, and a few H.E. were fired on the Support trench by CHALK PIT WOOD. These caused
little damage to the trench. Some T.M's were fired on POSEN ALLEY.

There were no Casualties in the Battalion under my Command. One officer and 3 O.R.
of the R.E. was slightly gassed, and 3 O.R. of R.E. killed.

I might mention, that owing to the delay of the Fatigue Party bringing up the Stores
for the Smoke Attack, arrangements were delayed and only just completed in time. Also the
"CODE message "ZEPPELIN LONDON" never reached me, and that "ZEPPELIN YORK" did not
reach my Signals until 7.15 p.m. It has been reported to me from every source that the men
of my Battalion carried out their duties in a satisfactory manner, and all the minor
arrangements made by the Battalion worked smoothly.

(Signd) W. Newton Lieut. Col.
Commanding 13th Bn East Surrey Regt.

1875 Wt. W593/826 1,000,000 4/15 J.B.C. & A. A.D.S.S./Forms/C. 2118.

120 e/o Vol 6

Lalbury 6.D.
9 sheets

VOLUME 6

WAR DIARY

~ OF ~

13TH BN EAST SURREY REGT.

FROM NOV. 1ST TO NOV. 30TH 1916

13ᵗʰ BATTALION
EAST SURREY REGIMENT

WAR DIARY
or
INTELLIGENCE SUMMARY.

(Erase heading not required)

Instructions regarding War Diaries and Intelligence
Summaries are contained in F. S. Regs. Part II.
and the Staff Manual respectively. Title pages
will be prepared in manuscript.

/20ᵗʰ INF. BRIGADE
40ᵗʰ DIVISION

Place	Date	Hour	Summary of Events and Information	Remarks and references to Appendices
AVERDOINGT. (DÉPARTEMENT PAS DE CALAIS)	1.11.16		Parades under Company arrangements.	(RNYE
	2.11.16		The Battalion marched to billets at REBREUVE and LA COUTURE via GOUY-EN-TERNOIS, MAGNICOURT-SUR-CANCHE and HOUVIN HOUVIGNEUL. Brigade Headquarters were established at the Château, REBREUVE.	Map Reference. LENS 11. 1/40,000 RNYE. RNYE.
REBREUVE	3.11.16		Parades under Company arrangements.	RNYE.
	4.11.16		The Battalion marched to billets at MEZEROLLES via NEUVILLETTE and BARLY. Brigade Headquarters were established at REMAISNIL.	(RNYE.
MEZEROLLES (DÉPARTEMENT DE LA SOMME.)	5.11.16		The Battalion marched to billets at VACQUERIE and DOMESMONT via LE MEILLARD and BERNAVILLE. Headquarters A,B+C Companies were billeted in VACQUERIE and D Company in DOMESMONT. Brigade Headquarters were established at RIBEAUCOURT.	RNYE.
VACQUERIE	6.11.16		Parades under Company arrangements.	RNYE.

2353 Wt. W2544/1454 700,000 5/15 D. D. & L.   A.D.S.S. Forms/C 2118.

Army Form C. 2118.

WAR DIARY

or

INTELLIGENCE SUMMARY.

(Erase heading not required.)

13ᵗʰ BATTALION
EAST SURREY REGIMENT

Instructions regarding War Diaries and Intelligence
Summaries are contained in F. S. Regs., Part II.
and the Staff Manual respectively. Title pages
will be prepared in manuscript.

/20ᵗʰ INF. BRIGADE
40ᵗʰ DIVISION

Place.	Date	Hour	Summary of Events and Information	Remarks and references to Appendices
VACQUERIE	7·11·16		The Phases of the attack were practiced by Companies.	9·A·7/t.
	8·11·16		Parades under Company arrangements	9·N·7/t
	9·11·16		The Battalion practiced the attack	9·N·7/t
	10·11·16		Brigade Field Day — The Brigade carried out an attack from VACQUERIE in the direction of RIBEAUCOURT.	9·N·7/t
	11·11·16		Parades under Company arrangements. The 40ᵗʰ Division became part of the 13ᵗʰ Corps, 5ᵗʰ Army. Nominal roll of officers is given in Appendix I.	
	12·11·16		The Battalion marched to billets at DOULLENS via FIENVILLERS, HARDINVAL and HEM. Brigade Headquarters were established at DOULLENS.	9·J·7/t. · 9·J·7/t.

2353 Wt. W2544/1454 700,000 5/15 D. D. & L.   A.D.S.S. Forms/C. 2118.

13ᵀᴴ BATTALION
EAST SURREY REGIMENT.

Army Form C. 2118.

WAR DIARY

or

INTELLIGENCE SUMMARY.

(Erase heading not required.)

Instructions regarding War Diaries and Intelligence
Summaries are contained in F. S. Regs., Part II.
and the Staff Manual respectively. Title pages
will be prepared in manuscript.

120ᵀᴴ INF. BRIGADE
40ᵀᴴ DIVISION

Place	Date	Hour	Summary of Events and Information	Remarks and references to Appendices
DOULLENS	13.11.16		Parades under Company arrangements.	Wⁿ ⁷ₗ
	14.11.16		The Battalion marched to SOUASTRE via MONDICOURT – PAS – HÉNU. The 120ᵗʰ Infantry Brigade became Brigade in Reserve to the 49ᵗʰ Division (3rd Army).	hori Refʳᵃ LENS II Troops. Wⁿ ⁷ₗ
SOUASTRE	15.11.16		The Battalion relieved the 4ᵗʰ Battⁿ Kings Own Yorkshire Light Infantry of the 148ᵗʰ Inf. Bde 49ᵗʰ Division 3ʳᵈ Army, in the left subsector HEBUTERNE. Headquarters were established on the Eastern edge of HEBUTERNE, on the SAILLY-AU-BOIS – PUISIEUX-AU-MONT Road. On our left was the 4ᵗʰ Battⁿ W. Ridings & the 147ᵗʰ Bde 49ᵗʰ Dvn 7ᵗʰ Corps 3rd Army. (The 13ᵗʰ Bⁿ East Surrey Regt being the left Battalion of the 5ᵗʰ Army). On our right was the 11ᵗʰ Battⁿ Kings Own Rd Regt. On completion of relief the 120ᵗʰ Infantry Bde came under the orders of the G.O.C. 31st Division.	Wⁿ-Mt.
HEBUTERNE	16.11.16		Situation fairly quiet. Throughout the day our heavy guns intermittently shelled the enemy's lines. The enemy sent a number of whizz bangs into THORPE ST.	Wⁿ-Mt.

2353 Wt. W²544/1454 700,000 5/15 D. D. & L. A.D.S.S. Forms/C. 2118.

Army Form C. 2118.

13ᵀᴴ BATTALION

EAST SURREY REGIMENT.

WAR DIARY

or

INTELLIGENCE SUMMARY.

(Erase heading not required.)

Title pages /28* Inf. Brigade
40ᵗʰ Division

Instructions regarding War Diaries and Intelligence
Summaries are contained in F. S. Regs. Part II.
and the Staff Manual respectively. Title pages
will be prepared in manuscript.

Place	Date	Hour	Summary of Events and Information	Remarks and references to Appendices
HEBUTERNE	17.11.16		Shells were exchanged throughout the day.	
			Casualties :- 1 or Killed. 1 or wounded	J.M.L.
	18.11.16		Situation normal. Wet weather caused the sides of the trenches to fall in where not reveted, consequently several communication trenches became almost impassable	
			Casualties :- 2 or wounded	J.M.L.
	19.11.16		Between 4 + 5 p.m. the enemy bombarded one of our advanced posts at the top of YUZ trench, with whizz bangs and aerial darts. Le S.M. R.T. PADGET went forward under heavy fire and rescued a number of men who had been buried in shelters	
			Casualties 1 or wounded.	J.M.L.
	20.11.16		Situation normal.	
			Casualties :- 2 or killed 5 or wounded (all caused on 19ᵗʰ by bombardment)	A.M.L.

2353   Wt. W2544/1454   700,000   5/15   D. D. & L.   A.D.S.S. Forms/C. 2118.

WAR DIARY

or

~~INTELLIGENCE~~ SUMMARY.

(Erase heading not required.)

13ᵗʰ Battalion
EAST SURREY REGIMENT.
Title pages /120ᵗʰ Infᵗʳʸ Brigade
40ᵗʰ Division

Instructions regarding War Diaries and Intelligence
Summaries are contained in F. S. Regs., Part II.
and the Staff Manual respectively. Title pages
will be prepared in manuscript.

Place	Date	Hour	Summary of Events and Information	Remarks and references to Appendices
HEBUTERNE	21·11·16		The Battalion was relieved by the 18ᵗʰ Battalion Durham Light Infantry (92 wds. Bde) and marched into camp (tents) at COUIN. The 120ᵗʰ Infantry Bde rejoined the 40ᵗʰ Division. Lieut F.N.CORBEN and 2ⁿᵈ Lieut W.V.B.HUGHES were evacuated sick to C.C.S.	J.H.N.H.L.
COUIN	22·11·16		The Battalion marched to AMPLIER via AUTHIE – THIÈVRES – ORVILLE and was billeted in huts.	J.H.N.H.L.
AMPLIER	23·11·16		The Battalion marched to billets in BONNEVILLE via DOULLENS – CANDAS.	J.H.N.H.L.
BONNEVILLE	24·11·16		The Battalion marched to billets in BUSSUS·BUSSUE via MONTRELET – BERNEUIL – DOMART – GORENFLOS. Brigade Headquarters were established at GORENFLOS. The 40ᵗʰ Division came under the orders of the 15ᵗʰ Corps 4ᵗʰ Army.	J.H.N.H.L.
BUSSUS	25·11·16		Resting & cleaning up.	J.H.N.H.L.

2353 Wt. W2544/1454 700,000 5/15 D. D. & L. A.D.S.S. Forms/C. 2118.

13th Battalion

EAST SURREY REGIMENT.

Army Form C. 2118.

WAR DIARY

or

~~INTELLIGENCE SUMMARY.~~

(Erase heading not required.)

Instructions regarding War Diaries and Intelligence Summaries are contained in F. S. Regs., Part II. and the Staff Manual respectively. Title pages 120th Inf. Brigade will be prepared in manuscript. 40th Division

Place	Date	Hour	Summary of Events and Information	Remarks and references to Appendices
BUSSUS	26.11.16		Battalion Church Parade.	M.M.Lt.
	27.11.16		Parades under Company arrangements.	M.M.Lt.
	28.11.16		Parades according to Battalion Programme of work. – musketry, arms & squad drill.	M.M.Lt.
	29.11.16		Do	M.M.Lt.
			Captain E. CROCKER reported back from the 1st Battn. East Surrey Regt.	
	30.11.16		Parades by companies.	M.M.Lt.
			The following promotions were notified in the London Gazette dated 27th November 1916. (Morning Post dated 28th November) Lt. Lieut C.R. BLACKBURNE to be temp: Capt. (29.8.16). temp: 2nd Lieut F. WLANHAM to be temp: Lieut (19.9.16). temp: 2nd Lieut V.W. SCOTT to be temp: Lieut. (6.10.16) temp: 2nd Lieut C.J. NORRES to be temp: Lieut (29.8.16)	M.M.Lt.

M. Murrum Lt. Colonel.
Commanding 13th Battn. East Surrey Regiment.

2353 Wt. W2544/1454 700,000 5/15 D. D. & L. A.D.S.S. Forms/C. 2118.

Army Form C. 2118.

WAR DIARY

or

INTELLIGENCE SUMMARY.

(Erase heading not required.)

Instructions regarding War Diaries and Intelligence
Summaries are contained in F. S. Regs., Part II.
and the Staff Manual respectively. Title pages
will be prepared in manuscript.

Place	Date	Hour	Summary of Events and Information	Remarks and references to Appendices

Roll of Officers serving with the Battalion on 11th November 1916.

Headquarters
Lt.Col.W.C. Newton. (C.O.) ---- Major E.B. Toole (3rd Dorsets)(2nd in command) ---- Lieut.F.S. Airey (Adjutant) ----
2nd Lieut.H.R. Hueton (Asst.Adjt + Signal Officer) ---- Lieut.F.S. Beecroft (Transport Officer) ---- Lieut.F.J. Hann (Lewis Gun Officer) ----
2nd Lieut.F.W. Lanham (Bombing Officer) ---- Capt.G.R. Spence (Medical Officer) ---- Capt.W.H. Spinney (Chaplain) ----
(Qm) Lieut.F. Foulon (Quartermaster) ---- No.3200. E. Seymour (Regt. Sgt. Major) ---- No.5104. F. Tablet (Regt. Qr. Mash Sgt)

"A" Company
Major R.S. Taylor. (O.C.) ---- Lieut. R.H. Hunter ---- Lieut. F. Davis ----
2nd Lieut. R.H.W. King ---- 2nd Lieut. E.E. Dodd ---- 2nd Lieut. C.P.S. Cooper ----
Lieut. C.R. Blackburne ---- 2nd Lieut. A.L. Anderson ----

"B" Company
Capt. C.E. Linge (O.C.) ---- 2nd Lieut. G.R. Alexander ---- 2nd Lieut. A.C. Thompson ----
2nd Lieut. F. Menzies-Jones ----
2nd Lieut. G.D. Dieset ----

"C" Company
Capt. H.P. Taunton. (O.C.) ---- 2nd Lieut. F.W. Hueton ---- 2nd Lieut. W.H.C. Brinkley ----
2nd Lieut. M.W. Hagger ---- 2nd Lieut. W.T.D. Hughes ---- 2nd Lieut. G.S. Drew ----
2nd Lieut. C. Johnston ----

"D" Company
Capt. L.B. Mills. (OC) ---- Lieut. F.W. Corker ---- 2nd Lieut. L.J. Deacon ----
2nd Lieut. C.M. James ---- 2nd Lieut. A.W. Gill ---- 2nd Lieut. W. A. Morris ----

2353   Wt. W2544/1454   700,000   5/15   D. D. & L.   A.D.S.S. Forms/C. 2118.

7. D.
sheet

Confidential

War Diary.

13th Battn East Surrey Regiment.

Volume 7

1st December 1916 — 31st December 1916.

13th Battalion

EAST SURREY REGIMENT

WAR DIARY

or

INTELLIGENCE SUMMARY.

(Erase heading not required.)

Instructions regarding War Diaries and Intelligence
Summaries are contained in F. S. Regs., Part II.
and the Staff Manual respectively. Title pages
will be prepared in manuscript.

28th Inf. Brigade
40th Division.

Place	Date	Hour	Summary of Events and Information	Remarks and references to Appendices
BUSSUS	1.12.16		Training carried out according to the Battalion Programme. Lieut C.J.NOAKES (11.11.16) + Capt C.R.BLACKBURNE (28.11.16) were evacuated sick to England.	A.W.J.
	2.12.16		Parades according to Battalion Programme.	A.W.J.
	3.12.16		Battalion Church Parade.	A.W.J.
	4.12.16		Platoon & Company training continued	A.W.J.
	5.12.16		Do	A.W.J.
	6.12.16		Do	A.W.J.
	7.12.16		Captain O.G.NORMAN reported for duty. (from 1st Bn East Surrey Regt.)	A.W.J.

2353 Wt. W3544/1454 700,000 5/15 D. D. & L. A.D.S.S. Forms/C 2118.

13ᵗʰ Battalion

EAST SURREY REGIMENT.

Army Form C. 2118.

WAR DIARY

or

~~INTELLIGENCE SUMMARY.~~

(Erase heading not required.)

Instructions regarding War Diaries and Intelligence Summaries are contained in F. S. Regs., Part II. and the Staff Manual respectively. Title pages will be prepared in manuscript.

120ᵗʰ Inf. Brigade
40ᵗʰ Division

Place	Date	Hour	Summary of Events and Information	Remarks and references to Appendices
BUSSUS	8.12.16		Platoon & Company training	Mₐₕₙᵧₑ.
	9.12.16		D⁰	Mₐₕₙᵧₑ.
			Major R.S.TAYLOR was appointed (temporarily) Camp Commandant 40ᵗʰ Division	
	10.12.16		Battalion Church Parade.	Mₐₕₙᵧₑ.
	11.12.16		Firing on the rifle range W of BUSSUS.	Mₐₕₙᵧₑ.
	12.12.16		D⁰	Mₐₕₙᵧₑ.
	13.12.16		D⁰	Mₐₕₙᵧₑ.
	14.12.16		The Battalion marched to PONT REMY and billeted there.	Mₐₕₙᵧₑ.

2353 Wt. W2544/1454 700,000 5/15 D. D. & L. A.D.S.S. Forms/C 2116.

13th Battalion
EAST SURREY REGIMENT

Army Form C. 2118.

WAR DIARY

or

INTELLIGENCE SUMMARY.

(Erase heading not required.)

Instructions regarding War Diaries and Intelligence
Summaries are contained in F. S. Regs., Part II.
and the Staff Manual respectively. Title pages
will be prepared in manuscript.

120 Infantry Brigade
40th Division

Place	Date	Hour	Summary of Events and Information	Remarks and references to Appendices
PONT REMY	16.12.16		The Battalion entrained at PONT REMY Station & proceeded to Edge Hill Station near DERNANCOURT. After detraining the Battalion marched to huts in Camp 112 situated on the BRAY-MEAULTÉ Road. Lieut F.N. CORDEN returned from Hospital. 2/Lieut. C.T. de BEAUREPAIRE reported for duty.	AN.T.
Camp 112	17.12.16		All available men were employed drawing & clearing up the Camp.	AN.T.
			After Church Parade Brigadier General the Hon C.S. DRUMMOND-WILLOUGHBY C.M.G. presented Coy. Sergt. Major R.T.PADGET with a D.C.M. ribbon.	AN.T.
	18.12.16		Draining & clearing the Camp.	AN.T.
	19.12.16		D°	AN.T.
	20.12.16		D°	AN.T.

2353 Wt. W2544/1454 700,000 5/15 D. D. & L.   A.D.S.S. Forms/C. 2118.

13th Battalion
EAST SURREY REGT.

WAR DIARY
or
INTELLIGENCE SUMMARY.

(Erase heading not required.)

Army Form C. 2118.

Instructions regarding War Diaries and Intelligence
Summaries are contained in F. S. Regs., Part II.
and the Staff Manual respectively. Title pages
will be prepared in manuscript.

120th Inf. Brigade
40th Division

Place	Date	Hour	Summary of Events and Information	Remarks and references to Appendices
CAMP 112	21/12/16		A Works Battalion was formed by the 40th Division. Capt. O.G. NORMAN + 50 other ranks were sent to it from this Battalion.	J.M.N.B.
	22/12/16		Parades under Company arrangements.	J.M.N.B.
	23/12/16		D°	J.M.N.B.
	24/12/16		Church Parade. A successful Battalion Concert was held in the evening.	J.M.N.B.
	25/12/16		Church Parade. A cinematograph Performance was arranged by the Chaplain. CAPT. C.R. BLACKBURNE returned from sick leave.	J.M.N.B.
	26/12/16		120th Infantry Brigade relieved the 100th Infantry Brigade. BOUCHAVESNES NORTH. The 13th Batn East Surrey Regt. proceeded by lorries to MAUREPAS HALTE, thence on foot to Brigade support where they relieved the 9th Bn H.L.I. Each Battalion consisted of 20 officers + 600 men. The remainder formed Details + proceeded by lorries to Camp 20 near SUZANNE (A27 d.) The 13th Divn transport was Brigaded at A23d.	J.M.N.B.

2353 Wt. W2544/1454 700,000 5/15 D. D. & L. A.D.S.S. Forms/C. 2118.

13th Battalion

EAST SURREY REGT.

WAR DIARY
or
INTELLIGENCE SUMMARY.

(Erase heading not required.)

Army Form C. 2118.

Instructions regarding War Diaries and Intelligence
Summaries are contained in F. S. Regs., Part II. and the Staff Manual respectively. Title pages will be prepared in manuscript.

Part II. 10th Inf. Brigade
40th Division.

Place	Date	Hour	Summary of Events and Information	Remarks and references to Appendices
				War Rept
BOUCHAVESNES	27.12.16		The Battalion occupied dugouts in a valley near B16d 4.7. Large parties were occupied laying trench boards from the valley to AGILE AVENUE.	ALBERT/4000 1st Section M.O.'g.
	28.12.16		Do	M.O.'g.
			Situation quiet.	
	29.12.16		Do	M.O.'g.
	30.12.16		(2nd in Comd) The Battalion relieved the 14th H.L.I. occupying the left subsection B Company came under the O.C. 14th Argyll Sutherland Hrs. & relieved his right Company. This Company was then on the extreme right of the British line. The 77th Infantry Regiment (French) occupied the next sector. Throughout the day there was intermittent shelling on both sides — chiefly shrapnel. 2nd Lieut A.W. NEWMAN and T.B. MILLS reported for duty from 10th East Surrey Regt. Lieut F.N. COREE(?) was admitted to Field Ambulance (sick).	M.O.'g.

2353   Wt. W2544/1454 700,000 5/15 D. D. & L.   A.D.S.S. Forms/C. 2118.

13th Battalion
EAST SURREY REGT.

WAR DIARY

or

INTELLIGENCE SUMMARY

(Erase heading not required.)

Army Form C. 2118.

Instructions regarding War Diaries and Intelligence
Summaries are contained in F. S. Regs., Part II.
and the Staff Manual respectively. Title pages
will be prepared in manuscript.

120th Inf Bride
40th Division

Place	Date	Hour	Summary of Events and Information	Remarks and references to Appendices
BOUCHAVESNES NORTH	31.12.16	2.45 pm	The 120th Infantry Brigade was relieved by the 121st Infantry Bde in BOUCHAVESNES NORTH. The 13th Bn. East Surrey Regt. was relieved by the 20th Bn Middlesex Regt. Owing to the mud and water the communication trenches were impassable and the time taken in getting from the front line to MAUREPAS was at least 7 hours from MAUREPAS the Battalion proceeded in lorries to Camp 21 on the SUZANNE – MAREOURT Road. Casualties 1 ot. wounded.	(M.B.)

M. Thurston Lieut Colonel
Commanding 13th Batton East Surrey Regt.

1/1/17.

2353   Wt. W2544/1454   700,000   5/15   D. D. & L.   A.D.S.S. Forms/C. 2118.

Original

War Diary

of the

13th Battalion East Surrey Regiment

Volume 8.

1st January 1917 to 31st January 1917.

13th BATTALION

EAST SURREY REGT.

WAR DIARY

or

INTELLIGENCE SUMMARY.

(Erase heading not required.)

Instructions regarding War Diaries and Intelligence Summaries are contained in F. S. Regs., Part II. and the Staff Manual respectively. Title pages 120th Infantry Brigade 40th Division.
will be prepared in manuscript.

Place	Date	Hour	Summary of Events and Information	Remarks and references to Appendices
CAMP 21 MARICOURT.	1.1.17		The Battalion arrived at Camp 21 during the early hours of the morning. The last Company which, owing to the mud and the intense darkness had been obliged to spend the night at ANDOVER PLACE, did not arrive until 9 am. Casualties 1 or killed in BRAY on 28.12.16.	Appx 4.
	2/3.1.17		As the men had come back, covered in mud, from the trenches, these days were spent in cleaning up.	Appx 5.
	4.1.17		The 120th Inf. Brigade relieved the 119th Inf. Brigade in the RANCOURT Section. The 13th East Surreys relieved the 18th Welsh in the left subsection. On our left was the 2nd Battn. Scottish Rifles (33rd Inf Brigade 11th Division) – on our right the 11th Battn. Kings Own R.L. Regt. It was not possible to reach the front line during the day owing to the absence of trenches. The front line consisted of a number of posts held by Lewis guns & a few men. Situation quiet except for occasional interchanges of shells between the enemy & our artillery.	Appx 6.

2353   Wt. W2544/1454   700,000   5/15   D. D. & L.   A.D.S.S. Forms/C. 2118.

WAR DIARY
or
INTELLIGENCE SUMMARY.

(Erase heading not required.)

13th Battn. East Surrey Regt.
120th Inf. Brigade
40th Division

Instructions regarding War Diaries and Intelligence Summaries are contained in F. S. Regs., Part II. and the Staff Manual respectively. Title pages will be prepared in manuscript.

Place	Date	Hour	Summary of Events and Information	Remarks and references to Appendices
RANCOURT	5/1/17		The enemy shelled RANCOURT with 5.9 + 4.2s but did little damage. Capt R.D. Pirie proceeded to England on leave Officers course distinct.	M.Fg.
	6/1/17		Company reliefs were successfully carried out. B Coy relieved C Coy in the left subsector. D Coy relieved A Coy in the right subsector. During the day our artillery shelled enemy frontage in ST PIERRE VAAST WOOD.	M.Fg.
	7/1/17		The enemy shelled Battalion Headquarters with 77mm + RANCOURT with 5.9. Our artillery retaliated on ST PIERRE VAAST WOOD. 2nd Lieut Wm R. Hughes returned from C.C.I.	M.Fg.
	8/1/17		The Battalion was relieved by the 14th H.L.I. moved into Brigade Reserve at MAUREPAS where tents in camp R were occupied. Casualties 1 or killed 1 or wounded. Major E.G. Park (3rd Dorset) was attached with B Col.	M.Fg.

2353 Wt. W.3541/1454 700,000 5/15 D. D. & L.   A.D.S.S./Forms/C. 2118.

Army Form C. 2118.

12th Battalion
East Surrey Regt.

WAR DIARY
or
INTELLIGENCE SUMMARY.

(Erase heading not required.)

Instructions regarding War Diaries and Intelligence Summaries are contained in F. S. Regs., Part II. and the Staff Manual respectively. Title pages will be prepared in manuscript.

120th Inf Brigade
40th Division

Place	Date	Hour	Summary of Events and Information	Remarks and references to Appendices
MAUREPAS	9.1.17		2nd Lieut. L Rutherford & R.M. Meadows reported for duty.	
	11.1.17		Various improvements to Camp.	
	12.1.17		The 120th Infantry Brigade marched by the 120th Inf Bde. The 12th Railways were relieved by the 21st Railways moved to Camp 21. Casualties 1 or wounded	
CAMP 21 MARICOURT	13.1.17		Cleaning up & improving the Camp in the direction of the Camp Commandant	
	15.1.17		2nd Lieut PP Print proceeds to Frs Ambulance (Sick)	
	16.1.17		Considerable improvement made to the Camp.	
	18.1.17		The 120th Inf Bde relieved the 119th Inf Bde in BOUCHAVESNES NORTH Sector. The 13th Railways relieved the 12th & W.R. in the left subsector. On our right was the 11th Bn. K.O.R. & on our left 13th Bn Yorks (121st Inf Bde). Two companies occupied the front line with one	

2353 Wt. W2344/1454 700,000 5/15 D. D. & L. A.D.S.S./Forms/C. 2118.

13th Battalion
East Surrey Regt.

WAR DIARY

or

INTELLIGENCE SUMMARY.

(*Erase heading not required.*)

120th Inf Brigade
40th Division

Instructions regarding War Diaries and Intelligence
Summaries are contained in F. S. Regs., Part II.
and the Staff Manual respectively. Title pages
will be prepared in manuscript.

Place	Date	Hour	Summary of Events and Information	Remarks and references to Appendices
BOUCHAVESNES NORTH	18/1/17	etc.	in support and one in Reserve at ANDOVER PLACE. Lieut D.W. Scott returned from R&T.	18/1/17
	19/1/17		Our artillery heavily shelled the enemy support & front lines. The enemy retaliated with 77 mm + 5.9. on our front line. Between 9 p.m. & 11.30 p.m. the enemy dropped between five & hundred gas shells into ANDOVER PLACE. Casualties 4 or wounded.	19/1/17
	20/1/17		The enemy shelled our front & support lines at intervals throughout the day in reply to our artillery fire. A considerable number of aerial starts were fired at our left Company front, apparently for registration purpose. Company which were completed. Casualties 3 or killed.	20/1/17
	21/1/17		At dawn a large number of the enemy were seen evacuating advanced posts and lines upon by our artillery. During the day our artillery were more active than usual. Casualties 1 or wounded.	21/1/17

2353 Wt. W.2344/1454 700,000 3/15 D. D. & L. A.D.S.S./Forms/C. 2118.

WAR DIARY

or

INTELLIGENCE SUMMARY.

(Erase heading not required.)

13th Battalion
East Surrey Regt.

Instructions regarding War Diaries and Intelligence
Summaries are contained in F. S. Regs., Part II.
and the Staff Manual respectively. Title pages *120th Inf Brig*
will be prepared in manuscript. *40th Division*

Place	Date	Hour	Summary of Events and Information	Remarks and references to Appendices
BOUCHAVESNES NORTH	22.1.17		The Battalion was relieved by the 14th Bn H.L.I. moved into Brigade Support at	
			ASQUITH FLATS (GENIÈGE) where the it was accommodated in dug-outs.	
			Lt Col E.C Atkins 4th Leicester Regt now attached assumed command.	G.R.N.H.
			Lieut. J.S Davis reported to the R.T.O. as an observer (for probation)	
ASQUITH FLATS	23.1.17		Casualties 1 or 2 wounded.	G.R.N.H.
	24.1.17		Work on dug outs & duck board tracks.	G.R.N.H.
	26.1.17		The 120 Inf Bde was relieved by the 24th Inf Bde (8th Division). The 13th East Surreys were relieved by the 2nd East Lancs, & proceeded by lorries to Camp 1st near SAILLY LAURETTE. Details evacuated Camp 20 marched to Camp 12.	G.R.N.H.
	27.1.17		The Battalion (excluding Details) marched to CORBIE where it was billeted in Area C	G.R.N.H.
			2nd Lieut C.S Fisher Jones was evacuated sick to C.C.S.	

2353 Wt. W 2544/1454 700,000 5/15 D. D. & L.   A.D.S.S./Forms/C. 2118.

13ᵗʰ Battalion
East Surrey Regᵗ

WAR DIARY

or

INTELLIGENCE SUMMARY.

(Erase heading not required.)

Instructions regarding War Diaries and Intelligence
Summaries are contained in F. S. Regs. Part II.
and the Staff Manual respectively. Title pages
will be prepared in manuscript.

120ᵗʰ Inf Bde
40ᵗʰ Division

Place	Date	Hour	Summary of Events and Information	Remarks and references to Appendices
CORBIE	28/4/17		During this period the men were reclothed & re-equipped. Fighting Platoons were organised & Recreational Training arranged.	

E. C. Arden
Lieut Colonel
Commanding 13ᵗʰ Battalion East Surrey Regiment

2333 Wt. W3541/1454 700,000 5/15 D. D. & L.   A.D.S.S./Forms/C. 2118.

No. 9

9. D.
3 sheet

War Diary

of the

13th Battalion East Surrey Regiment.

1st February 1917.

to

28th February 1917.

Volume 9.

WAR DIARY

or

INTELLIGENCE SUMMARY.

(Erase heading not required.)

13th Battalion
East Surrey Regt

Instructions regarding War Diaries and Intelligence
Summaries are contained in F. S. Regs., Part II.
and the Staff Manual respectively. Title pages
will be prepared in manuscript.

/20th Sub Bde
40th Division

Place	Date	Hour	Summary of Events and Information	Remarks and references to Appendices
CORBIE	Feb 1-9 1917		During this period the Battalion carried on training in bayonet fighting, physical exercise, handling arms, musketry & trench work. 2nd Lieut W F C Embley was evacuated sick to C.C.S. 9.2.17. whence he proceeded to England. 2nd Lieut A G de Beaurepaire reported for duty 5.2.17.	Why.
	Feb. 10.		The Battalion marched to Camp 111 on the MÉAULTE - BRAY Road.	W. Why.
CAMP 111	Feb 11		The Battalion marched to BRAY-TOURBIÈRE Railhead and took over working parties from the 13th Yorks. Regt. Headquarters were established at 4 Rue Carité, BRAY	W. Why.
BRAY-TOUR BIÈRE	Feb 12-23		All available men were employed unloading trains for the O.C. 217th Army Troops Cy R.E. 15th Corps Ammunition Officer & 15th Corps Ordnance Officer. 2nd Lieut W A Andrew reported for duty 14.2.17. 3 o.r. were killed on 14.2.17.	W. Why. L.B.
	Feb 24		The Battalion was relieved by the 19th Royal Welch Fus. & proceeded to Camp 21.	W. Why.
CAMP 21.	Feb 25-28		Training was carried on in accordance with the Battalion programme.	W. Why.

W. Winton Lt Col
Cmdg 13th Bn East Surrey Regiment

2353 Wt. W3547/454 700,000 5/15 D. D. & L. A.D.S.S./Forms/C. 2118.

Vol 10

120/240

E. M.

10. D
9 sheets

War Diary

OF THE

13TH Bn: Bn: East Surrey Regt.

VOLUME. 10

From 1st March 1917. To 31st March 1917:

confidential

Army Form C. 2118.

13th Battalion East Surrey Regt.   WAR DIARY

or

INTELLIGENCE SUMMARY.

(Erase heading not required.)

Instructions regarding War Diaries and Intelligence
Summaries are contained in F. S. Regs., Part II. /20th Inf. Brigade
and the Staff Manual respectively. Title pages
will be prepared in manuscript.   40th Division.

Place	Date	Hour	Summary of Events and Information	Remarks and references to Appendices
Camp 21 MARICOURT.	1/5.2.17		During this period Platoon & Company training was carried on in accordance with the Battalion Programme.	
			2nd Lt A.W Gill was evacuated sick to England on the 4th March.	M.M.Gt.
	6.3.17		The Battalion relieved the 1st Bn Middlesex Regt (98th Infantry Brigade 33rd Division) in Brigade Support (at ROAD WOOD) BETHUNE ROAD Sector. Headquarters were established at P.C MADAME (C 25 d 5.8)	Map Ref. BOUCHAVESNES 1/10000 Ed. 4A
			Capt. C.R BLACKBURNE and Lieut F.N CORBEN were evacuated sick to England.	M.M.Gt.
ROAD WOOD Sect. BOUCHAVESNES	7.3.17		The Battalion relieved the 4th Bn King's Liverpool Regt. in the left subsector BETHUNE ROAD. Headquarters were established at P.C MARJORIE (C 20 d 15.90). On our right was the 11th Bn. King's Own R.L. Regt. On our left was the 8th Division. The boundaries of our line were: Northern C 15 d 6.3 Southern C 20 d 6.2. The trenches generally were in a very bad condition & movements during the day were very restricted. The left & centre Companies could be reached only under cover of darkness. Rations were brought up by pack mule to within 100 yards of Battn. Headquarters.	M.M.Gt.

WAR DIARY
or
INTELLIGENCE SUMMARY.

(Erase heading not required.)

13th Battalion Essex Surrey Regt

Instructions regarding War Diaries and Intelligence
Summaries are contained in F. S. Regs., Part II.
and the Staff Manual respectively. Title pages
will be prepared in manuscript.

30 Inf Bde
46 Division

Place	Date	Hour	Summary of Events and Information	Remarks and references to Appendices
BETHUNE ROAD	8.3.17		Occasional shelling throughout the day. Casualties: 3 o.r. wounded.	W.H.E.
	9.3.17		Situation normal. A few medium minenwerfer shells were dropped in the centre Company's front. Casualties: 3 o.r. wounded. 2nd Lt. G.S. DREW was admitted to hospital sick.	W.H.E.
	10.3.17		On the night 10/11th the Battalion was relieved by the 14th Bn Argyll & Sutherland Highlanders and moved into Brigade Reserve at HOWITZER WOOD H3 b 5.0.	See Appx. B 63.1.P.2. W.H.E.
HOWITZER WOOD	11.3.17		During the afternoon about 200 4.2s & 5.9s were dropped in the vicinity of the Battalion dug outs but no casualties were caused. The front portion of D Coy's cooker was however hit and blown to pieces.	W.H.E.
	12.3.17		Situation quiet.	W.H.E.

2353 Wt. W2544/1454 700,000 5/15 D. D. & L. A.D.S.S. Forms/C 2118.

13th Bn East Surrey Regt.

Army Form C. 2118.

WAR DIARY

or

INTELLIGENCE SUMMARY.

(Erase heading not required.)

40th Bn S.A.P.Bde. 40th Division

Instructions regarding War Diaries and Intelligence
Summaries are contained in F. S. Regs., Part II.
and the Staff Manual respectively. Title pages
will be prepared in manuscript.

Place	Date	Hour	Summary of Events and Information	Remarks and references to Appendices
HOWITZER WOOD	13.3.17		On the night 13/14 the Battalion relieved the 14th Bn Argyll Sutherland Hrs. in the left subsector BETHUNE ROAD. Headquarters were at P.C. MARJORIE. On our right was the 14th Bn H.L.I. (centre subsector). On our left the 2nd Rifle Bde. The enemy heavily shelled the ration dump in BOUCHAVESNES Ravine but caused no casualties. 2nd Lt. E.L.MORLEY and 2nd Lt. F.L.WARLAND reported for duty.	W.Wt.
BETHUNE ROAD	14.3.17		Between midnight the Battalion Headquarters were shelled with 4.2's. One shell burst at the entrance to the dug out killing R.I.M. SEYMOUR.E. and 3 Argylls. 2nd Lt. E.E.DODD was admitted to hospital sick.	W.Wt.
	15.3.17		During the night the enemy shelled the support trenches of the front line Companies & was more active than usual with Very lights. Casualties: 1 o.r. killed + 3 o.r. wounded. 2nd Lt R.N.GOODYEAR and 2nd Lt. N.F.BARLOW reported for duty.	

Cont'd.

2353 Wt. W2344/1454. 700,000 5/15 D. D. & L. A.D.S.S. Forms/C 2118.

WAR DIARY

or

INTELLIGENCE SUMMARY.

(Erase heading not required.)

13th Battalion East Surrey Regt.
/120th Inf Bde
40th Division

Instructions regarding War Diaries and Intelligence Summaries are contained in F. S. Regs., Part II. and the Staff Manual respectively. Title pages will be prepared in manuscript.

Place	Date	Hour	Summary of Events and Information	Remarks and references to Appendices
BETHUNE ROAD	16.3.17 ctd.		120th Infantry Bde Order No 81 was received giving instructions regarding the action to be taken in case of a voluntary withdrawal by the enemy. The 120th Infantry Brigade in conjunction with the advance of the 25th Inf Bde on its left, and taking the initiative from their troops would occupy the successive steps in echelon from N. to S. DETVA trench, DETVA support and BROUSSE trench. The 13th Bn E Surrey Regt taking the initiative from the Brigade on its left would move forward to the line C22 c 9.9 exclusive — C27 t 30.05 exclusive. Anticipatory orders were issued accordingly. During the night many patrols were sent out but all reported the enemy's line occupied.	[initials]
	16.3.17		On the night 16/17 March the Battalion was relieved by the 14th Bn Argyll & Sutherland Hrs. Headquarters or A and D Companies moved to LITTLEDALE BARRACKS. B & C Companies moved to HOWITZER WOOD. Casualties No 13774 Pte CLARK W missing 1 or wounded.	[initials]

13th Battalion East Surrey Regt.

Army Form C. 2118.

WAR DIARY
or
INTELLIGENCE SUMMARY.
(Erase heading not required.)

Instructions regarding War Diaries and Intelligence
Summaries are contained in F. S. Regs., Part II.
and the Staff Manual respectively. Title pages
will be prepared in manuscript.

/20ᵗʰ Inf. Bde.
40ᵗʰ Division.

Place	Date	Hour	Summary of Events and Information	Remarks and references to Appendices
HOWITZER WOOD.	17.3.17		At dusk the 14ᵗʰ Bn. Argyll Sutherland Hᵈʳˢ sent out patrols which reported the enemy lines unoccupied. They therefore moved forward and established themselves in the enemy third line of trenches. Casualties: 2ⁿᵈ Lt. N W HAGGER wounded 2 o.r. wounded.	Whʳʳ
	18.3.17	5.30 a.m.	Battalion Headquarters A Coy + Dᵒ Coy. moved to ROMADAME (ROAD WOOD).	Whʳʳ
		11 a.m.	B+C Companies under Lt. Col. E.C.ATKINS moved to the old quarry MARTORIE. Situation very quiet.	
ROAD WOOD	19.3.17	9 a.m.	The Battalion received orders to be in readiness to move at 10 minutes notice. Map Refs.	62c N W Section 4A
		2 p.m.	The Battalion assembled at the CRATER – BETHUNE ROAD in artillery formation. The Commanding Officer (Lt. Col. W.E.NEWTON) then detailed orders as to disposition return re.	
		3 p.m.	The Companies proceeded to take up an outpost line extending from I 10 x 4.3 to C 29 c 1.6 – East of ALLAINES and HAUT ALLAINES. Disposition A Coy on right C Coy on left B & Coy right support + Dᵒ Coy left support.	

WAR DIARY
or
INTELLIGENCE SUMMARY.

(Erase heading not required.)

13th East Surrey Regt.

F.S. Regs., Part II./20th Inf Bde

for Division

Instructions regarding War Diaries and Intelligence Summaries are contained in F. S. Regs., Part II. and the Staff Manual respectively. Title pages will be prepared in manuscript.

Place	Date	Hour	Summary of Events and Information	Remarks and references to Appendices
ROAD WOOD	19.3.17 da		Headquarters were established in ALLAINES (I4 a 70). Brigade Headquarters occupied P.C. MARTORIE. On our left was the 14th Bn Argyll Sutherland Hds. + on our right 20th Bn. Middlesex Regt. (commanded by Lt. Col. F.S.B. JOHNSON) Keenness and enthusiasm was very marked in having freed over French + through villages occupied by the enemy only 24 hours before. The Transport moved from PRISEBEND to CLERY whence rations were carried by pack mule to ALLAINES.	M.W.T.
ALLAINES	20.3.17	3 p.m.	The Battalion was relieved by the 19th Bn Welch Regt. and moved via FEUILLAUCOURT and CLERY to LINGER CAMP - CURLU A 30 d.1.5. Details Transport and Ord stores joined the Battalion at this camp.	M.W.T.
CURLU	21.3.17		The Battalion became A.Corps Reserve.	M.W.T.
CURLU	22/31.3.17		The Battalion was employed making a railway from MARICOURT to FERME ROUGE, under direction of the Railway Construction Engineer 4th Army. Brigade Headquarters moved to HOWITZER WOOD on the 22nd March. Lieut LA SEELEY and 2nd Lt. FR. WOODWARD reported for duty, 22.3.17	

2353 Wt. W2544/1454 700,000 5/15 D. D. & L. A.D.S.S. Forms/C. 2118.

13ª Battalion East Surrey Regt.

Army Form C. 2118.

WAR DIARY

or

~~INTELLIGENCE SUMMARY.~~

(*Erase heading not required.*)

Instructions regarding War Diaries and Intelligence 13ᵗʰ Bn Inf Bde
Summaries are contained in F. S. Regs., Part II. 40ᵗʰ Division.
and the Staff Manual respectively. Title pages
will be prepared in manuscript.

Place	Date	Hour	Summary of Events and Information	Remarks and references to Appendices
CURLU	24.3.17		Summer time was adopted : 11 pm became midnight.	
	25.3.17		The 40 Division moved into 15 Corps Reserve.	
	29.3.17		2nd Lt. E.E. DODD returned from hospital.	M.N.H.
	30.3.17		2nd Lt. E.L. MORLEY was admitted to hospital sick.	

W. Newton   Lieut Colonel
Comdg 13ᵗʰ Bn East Surrey Regiment.

2353   Wt. W2544/1454 700,000 5/15   D. D. & L.   A.D.S.S. Forms/C. 2118.

OPERATION ORDER   SECRET.

by

Lt. Col. W. Newton, Cmdg, 13th Bn E. Surr. Regt.

15/3/17.

1.   In case of a voluntary withdrawal
by the enemy on our front, touch is to
be maintained & all trenches vacated
by him are to be occupied.

2.   Should the Division on our left
move forward, this Brigade will
co-operate - the Bn in the Left Sub-
Sector - 13th E. Surr. Regt. - taking the
initiative from the Brigade on its
left - will move forward to the line
C. 22. c. 9. 9 exclusive - C. 27. b. 30.
05. exclusive with "D" Coy on Left -
"B" Coy in Centre - "A" Coy on Right
& "C" Coy in Support.   This
advance will be made in successive
steps in Echelon from North to
South - DETVA TRENCH - DETVA
SUPPORT - and BROUSSE TRENCH -
by Platoons.   The 14th N.F. J
will co-operate on our Right &
the 14th A. & S. H will be in
support in our old line.

3.   MACHINE GUNS.
        Two Machine Guns will be
placed at the disposal of the O.C.

? 13th Bn E. Surr Regt. They
will move with the SUPPORT COY.

R.E.

One Section 231st Field Coy R.E.
will be at disposal of O.C 13th Bn
E. Surr. Regt.

CONSOLIDATION.

New Positions will be consolidated
and Patrols pushed out along
the whole Front.

FLARES.

All units moving forward will
carry flares for communicating
position to Aircraft.

PRECAUTIONS.

Special precautions to be taken
to guard against land Mines or
other traps left by the enemy.

Some R.E. will be attached to
each Company to deal with
suspicious objects.

DRESS

Each man will be in fighting
order & will carry one extra
bandolier of S.A.A., full day's
ration and filled Water Bottle.
Bombing Sections will carry
boxes of bombs.

BATTN. H.Q.

Battalion H.Q. will move forward in rear of junction of LEFT and CENTRE COYS, commencing with "D" Coys present H.Q.

LEWIS GUNS.

All panniers & magazines will be carried forward.

Bamford
Lt + a/Lt.
13th Bn E. Surr Rgt.

Vol XI

War Diary

OF THE

13ᵗʰ Bⁿ B. East Surrey Regt.

VOLUME. II.

From 1ˢᵗ April 1917. To 30ᵗʰ April. 1917.

Army Form C. 2118.

WAR DIARY
or
INTELLIGENCE SUMMARY.
(Erase heading not required.)

12th R. Sur. Survey Regt.

Instructions regarding War Diaries and Intelligence
Summaries are contained in F. S. Regs., Part II.
and the Staff Manual respectively. Title pages
will be prepared in manuscript.

120th Inf. Brigade
40th Division

Place	Date	Hour	Summary of Events and Information	Remarks and references to Appendices
CURLU	1.4.17 to 15.4.17		During this period the Battalion was employed on the MARICOURT – FERME-ROUGE – PERONNE Railway under the 4th Army Railway Construction Engineer.	
	3.4.17		Lt. Col. E.C. ATKINS 2/5th Bn. Leicester Regt. proceeded to the Senior Officers' Course, Aldershot.	
	7.4.17		Capt. L.B. MILLS returned from the Senior Officers' Course, Aldershot.	
	9.4.17		2nd Lt. G.S. DREW returned from hospital.	
	10.4.17		2nd Lt. E.L. MORLEY returned from hospital.	
	11.4.17		2nd Lt. D.H.J.M. PLAGE was evacuated to England sick.	
	15.4.17		2nd Lt. W.A. ANDREW was evacuated to Field Ambulance sick. Lt. Col. W.C. NEWTON proceeded to FLIXECOURT to attend Commanding Officers Conference at the 4th Army School. Capt. L.B. MILLS assumed command of the Battalion.	M.M.L.S.
	16.4.17		The Battalion marched to EQUANCOURT via CLERY = ALLAINES = HAUT ALLAINES = MOISLAINS – MANANCOURT – ETRICOURT. Shelter was found in the remains of the village which had been almost completely destroyed by the retreating enemy.	M.M.L.S.

2353 Wt. W3544/1454 700,000 5/15 D. D. & L.   A.D.S.S./Forms/C. 2118.

1ᵈ Bⁿ. Bⁿ East Surrey Regt.

Instructions regarding War Diaries and Intelligence
Summaries are contained in F. S. Regs., Part II.
and the Staff Manual respectively. Title pages
will be prepared in manuscript.

120ᵗ Infantry Bde
40ᵗ Division.

Place	Date	Hour	Summary of Events and Information	Remarks and references to Appendices
EQUANCOURT	17.4.17		The Battalion rested at EQUANCOURT.	W.H.G.
	18.4.9		On the night of the 18/19ᵗʰ the Battalion relieved the 20ᵗʰ Bⁿ Middlesex Regt. 121ᵗʰ Inf Bde, left Brigade, centre Division, 15ᵗʰ Corps.	Map Ref⁵ 57ᶜ.S.E. G.3.A. 1/20000
			In the right subsector, left Brigade, centre Division, 15ᵗʰ Corps. The disposition were as follows: Battalion Headquarters in the sunken road at Q.28.c.2.6. A, B & D Companies in GOUZEAUCOURT WOOD and C Company in the sunken road at Q.23.c, with small post in front.	
			On our right were the 119ᵗʰ Brigade, on our left the 11ᵗʰ R.K.O.Y.L. Regt. There were no trenches in this subsector – the men being accommodated in bivouacs and small shelters.	W.H.G.
GOUZEAUCOURT WOOD	19.4.17		Situation fairly quiet. During the day the enemy dropped a number of 4.2.s in GOUZEAUCOURT WOOD presumably searching for our battery position. During the night a line of resistance was made with barbed wire along the north eastern edge of the wood.	W.H.G.
			Casualties 1 o.r. killed	

2353 Wt. W2344/1434 700,000 5/15 D. D. & L. A.D.S.S./Forms/C.2118.

Army Form C. 2118.

WAR DIARY
or
INTELLIGENCE SUMMARY.

(Erase heading not required.)

Instructions regarding War Diaries and Intelligence Summaries are contained in F. S. Regs., Part II. and the Staff Manual respectively. Title pages will be prepared in manuscript.

13th East Surrey Regt.
120th Inf Brigade
40th Division

Place	Date	Hour	Summary of Events and Information	Remarks and references to Appendices
GOUZEAUCOURT WOOD	20.4.17		Occasional shells were dropped in the wood throughout the day. A strong point was made South of the sunken road about Q 28 c 2.6.	
	21.4.17	12.30am	The Battalion was ordered to move forward in conjunction with the 119th Brigade on the right and the 11th R.KORL Regt. on the left and occupy a line from FIFTEEN RAVINE sectionn to Q 17 d 8.7 Patrols reconnoitred our objective but found no signs of the enemy. Strong posts were thereupon dug along the line.	
		4.20am	Under cover of our artillery barrage parties from D Coy advanced and occupied posts from FIFTEEN RAVINE to Q18c94, and from C Coy Q18c94 to Q17d87. One platoon of A Coy was attached to each of C & B Companies. A Coy (less 2 platoons) occupied the line of residences along the North Eastern edge of GOUZEAUCOURT WOOD. B Coy were in reserve at Q23 c 54. A small trench running from the sunken roads Q 23 c 54 to Q 23 a 86 was deepened and occupied by the remainder of C & D Companies. Casualties 3 or wounded.	

2353 Wt. W2544/1454 700,000 5/15 D. D. & L. A.D.S.S./Forms/C. 2118.

WAR DIARY

or

INTELLIGENCE SUMMARY.

(Erase heading not required.)

Instructions regarding War Diaries and Intelligence Summaries are contained in F.S. Regs., Part II. and the Staff Manual respectively. Title pages will be prepared in manuscript.

13th Bn East Surrey Regt

120th Inf Brigade

40th Division

Place	Date	Hour	Summary of Events and Information	Remarks and references to Appendices
GOUZEAUCOURT WOOD	22.4.17		Except for an occasional interchange of shells the situation was quiet. With a view to an attack on VILLERS PLOUICH it was proposed to capture the enemy strong point about Q.18.a.5.8. The 14th Bn Argyll & Sutherland Highlanders attempted to bomb down the enemy's trenches in Q.18.a.-t. but was unsuccessful. The operations on the enemy post Q.18.a.5.9 were therefore stopped. During the night a continuous trench about 4-5 feet deep was dug from FIFTEEN RAVINE to Q.17.d.8.7. Enemy snipers were very busy sniping several casualties. Casualties: 2nd Lt F.C. JOHNSTON, Lieut L.A. SEELEY, 2nd Lt F.C. WARRAND and 4 o.r. wounded	A. Wolfe.
	23.4.17		The enemy artillery were much more active shelling the sunken roads at Q.23.c.5.4., the track from there to QUEENS CROSS and GOUZEAUCOURT WOOD. Casualties 8 o.r. killed 9 o.r. wounded. Lieut F.C. JOHNSTON died of wounds.	A.Wolfe.

2353   Wt. W3541/1454   700,000   5/15   D. D. & L.   A.D.S.S./Forms/C. 2118.

13th R. East Surrey Regt.

WAR DIARY
or
INTELLIGENCE SUMMARY.

(Erase heading not required.)

Instructions regarding War Diaries and Intelligence 120 Inf. Brigade
Summaries are contained in F. S. Regs., Part II. 40th Division
and the Staff Manual respectively. Title pages
will be prepared in manuscript.

Place	Date	Hour	Summary of Events and Information	Remarks and references to Appendices
GOUZEAUCOURT WOOD	2.4.17		The 40th Division were ordered to assault the village of VILLERS PLOUICH and BEAUCAMP and gain a footing on the heights R.14 central and R.7 central. An account of how the Battalion captured VILLERS PLOUICH and reached its objectives is given on Appendix I. The Battalion went into action with 24 officers and 600 other ranks. Casualties:- Killed:- Capt. E. CROOKER, 2nd Lt. G. R. ALEXANDER, 2nd Lt. R. N. GOODYEAR and 26 other ranks. Missing:- 10 other ranks. Wounded:- Capt. L. B. MILLS, 2nd Lt. (A. Capt.) L. I. DEACON, 2nd Lt. H. WAIENMAN, 2nd Lt. R. M. MEADOWS, 2nd Lt. E. MORLEY, 2nd Lt. C. J. de BEAUREPAIRE, 2nd Lt. N. F. BARLOW, 2nd Lt. W. A. MORRIS (remained at duty) and 152 other ranks.	W.N.4t
VILLERS PLOUICH	2.4.17		The 11th R.KO.Y.L Regt. which had relieved the 14th Pn. A.I.N. captured BEAUCAMP and consolidated a position N.E. of the village.	

WAR DIARY

or

INTELLIGENCE SUMMARY.

(Erase heading not required.)

Instructions regarding War Diaries and Intelligence Summaries are contained in F. S. Regs., Part II. and the Staff Manual respectively. Title pages will be prepared in manuscript.

Place	Date	Hour	Summary of Events and Information	Remarks and references to Appendices

List of Officers who went into action on the morning of the 24th April 1917.

HEADQUARTERS.

Capt. L. B. Wills.
Capt. G. R. Skinner, R.A.M.C. M.O.
Lieut & Adjt. F. S. Ainger.
2nd Lieut. G. R. Prestor.

'A' COMPANY.

Lieut. F. J. Seaml.
2nd Lieut. R. M. Meadows.
2nd Lieut. P. L. Keeling.
3rd Lieut. R. N. Goodyear.
2nd Lieut. L. W. Newman.

'B' COMPANY.

Capt. E. Croxton.
2nd Lieut. P. J. de Beauvoars.
2nd Lieut. G. R. Alexander.
2nd Lieut. A. Thompson.

'C' COMPANY.

Capt. L. P. Harrison.
2nd Lieut. E. Morley.
2nd Lieut. F. W. Scott.
2nd Lieut. E. J. Drew.

'D' COMPANY.

Capt. L. S. Deacon.
2nd Lieut. N. A. Norris.
2nd Lieut. N. F. Barlow.
2nd Lieut. G. E. Deacon.
2nd Lieut. C. J. de Beauvoars.
2nd Lieut. C. M. James.
2nd Lieut. J. Rutherford.

13th East Surrey Regt.

WAR DIARY
or
INTELLIGENCE SUMMARY.
(Erase heading not required.)

Instructions regarding War Diaries and Intelligence Summaries are contained in F.S. Regs. Part II. and the Staff Manual respectively. Title pages will be prepared in manuscript.

1/20th ... Brigade
40 Division

Place	Date	Hour	Summary of Events and Information	Remarks and references to Appendices
			APPENDIX I.	
			The attack on VILLERS PLOUICH - 24th April 1917.	
			Objective: The Battalion was ordered to recapture VILLERS PLOUICH and form ... on the Right R7 central and R14 & 3 8 (Ravine).	
			The Battalion moved forward and occupied the trench from	
		2 a.m.	FIFTEEN RAVINE to Q17 & 87.	
			B Coy was on the Right, A Coy on the left, D Coy right support and C Coy left support.	
			Each man carried two sandbags and two bombs (hells No.5).	
			One platoon of C Coy (implatoon) of C Coy carried tools in the proportion of 3 shovels to 1 pick.	
		4.15am	Zero hour: The Battalion crept forward the enemy's ... our artillery barrage commenced. ... few ... rum rockets were sent up by the enemy and our artillery opened fire. The enemy line at this time was very erratic and caused little damage.	
		4.22am	The Battalion entered the enemy's trenches in Q.19 a ... after a	

Army Form C. 2118.

WAR DIARY
or
INTELLIGENCE SUMMARY.
(Erase heading not required.)

Instructions regarding War Diaries and Intelligence
Summaries are contained in F. S. Regs., Part II.
and the Staff Manual respectively. Title pages
will be prepared in manuscript.

13th East Surrey Regt.
120th Inf. Bde.
40th Division

Place	Date	Hour	Summary of Events and Information	Remarks and references to Appendices
			short struggle all resistance was overcome and the advance on	
			VILLERS PLOUICH continued. A good deal of trouble was caused by	
			enemy strong posts and machine gun emplacements but this was overcome	
			by the concentrated fire of Lewis guns and during attacks by bombers.	
		5.30am	On reaching the village the Battalion was split up into three parties,	
			the right being commanded by Capt E CROCKER, the centre by 2nd Lt G.R ALEXANDER	
			and the left by Capt H R NAUNTON.	
			After much opposition the right party reached its objective (the	
			Ravine in R Sound R14 central) At this junction Capt E CROCKER was	
			killed and Lt F. J. J. HANN took over command of the right party.	
			the centre party went through the left of the village and took up a	
			position on the hill about R7 centrals.	
			The left party stormed an enemy strong point on the VILLERS PLOUICH -	
			BEAUCAMP sunken road and after a sharp fight captured the enemy's	
			position and over 100 prisoners. It was then found that the village of	
			BEAUCAMP had not been captured by the Battalion on our left and that	

WAR DIARY
or
INTELLIGENCE SUMMARY.
(Erase heading not required.)

Instructions regarding War Diaries and Intelligence
Summaries are contained in F. S. Regs., Part II.
and the Staff Manual respectively. Title pages
will be prepared in manuscript.

Place	Date	Hour	Summary of Events and Information	Remarks and references to Appendices
			It was ordered to push on to the objective on R7. The position in the sunken road was then consolidated and a defensive flank thrown out to command BEAUCAMP together with the high ground to the East.	
		6.30am	Our barrage ceased + the work of consolidation progressed.	
		6.40am	The enemy opened very heavy fire with 4.2s + 5.9s on our centre and right parties. It was then decided to withdraw to available cover on the Eastern outskirts of the village. These two parties then joined together and the entrance to the village were covered with Lewis guns.	
		7.5am	Re 14th Bn R.F 2 reinforced the Battalion and another advance was made.	
		8 am	Capt. L B.MILLS (C.O) was wounded and command of the Battalion was assumed by Capt. H.P NAUNTON. Strong posts were established in R7 c+d and East of the Cemetery R11a.	
		8.30am	The enemy opened a terrific fire on VILLERS PLOUICH with 4.2s, 5.9s and 6-8" high explosive shells + shrapnel. The track running from the village through	

2353 Wt. W2544/1454 700,000 5/15 D. D. & L.   A.D.S.S./Forms/C. 2118.

Army Form C. 2118.

WAR DIARY

or

INTELLIGENCE SUMMARY.

(Erase heading not required.)

Instructions regarding War Diaries and Intelligence
Summaries are contained in F. S. Regs., Part II.
and the Staff Manual respectively. Title pages
will be prepared in manuscript.

Place	Date	Hour	Summary of Events and Information	Remarks and references to Appendices
		2 p.m.	Q18d received special attention. The bombardment slackened but the enemy kept up practical fire on the village and the entrances to it.	N.W.Lt.
			Estimated enemy casualties	
			Killed 2 officers 50 other ranks	
			Wounded + prisoners 4 " 300 "	
			6 officers 350 other ranks.	

W. Newton, Lt Col
Comdg 13th East Surrey Regt

2353 Wt. W2541/1454 700,000 5/15 D. D. & L.   A.D.S.S./Forms/C. 2118.

Army Form C. 2118.

13th Bn East Surrey Reg.
123rd Inf Brigade
40th Division

WAR DIARY
or
INTELLIGENCE SUMMARY.

(Erase heading not required.)

Instructions regarding War Diaries and Intelligence Summaries are contained in F. S. Regs., Part II. and the Staff Manual respectively. Title pages will be prepared in manuscript.

Place	Date	Hour	Summary of Events and Information	Remarks and references to Appendices
VILLERS PLOUICH	2.4.17	etc	At dusk the Battalion was relieved by the 13th Bn Yorks Regt. and proceeded to EQUANCOURT.	MHW/F
EQUANCOURT	26/30.4.17		The Battalion remained at EQUANCOURT. 24.4.17 Lt Col N C NEWTON returned from 4th Army School. 30.4.17 It was notified that Capt M J PEMBERTON had been struck off the establishment of the Battalion as from 22 Feby 1917. Casualties 3 on wounded (behind the line)	MHW/F

W. Newton Lieut Colonel
Cmdg 13th Bn East Surrey Reg.

2353 Wt. W2344/1454 700,000 5/15 D. D. & L. A.D.S.S./Forms/C. 2118.

13th Bn East Surrey Regiment.

Operation Order No. 48.

Ref. 57c S.E 8d 3A 1/40.000
Artillery Sketch. Barrages.

1. INFORMATION

The 40th Division will assault the Villages of VILLERS PLOUICH and BEAUCAMP. on the night 23/24th April.

119th Infy Bde will attack on the RIGHT.

120th " " " " " LEFT.

2. INTENTION

The Battalion will assault the Village of VILLERS PLOUICH, and gain a footing on the high ground to the N.E.

3. OBJECTIVE. Battalion Boundaries.

RIGHT BOUNDARY. from edge of 15 Ravine at R.19.a. 0.8 to R.14. b. 2.8.

LEFT BOUNDARY. from Q.18.c.3.6 to R.7. Central.

As soon as the objective has been gained the Battalion will consolidate on the Line R.7. Central to the Ravine R.14. b. 2. 8. (both inclusive)

4. STRONG POINTS.

Strong Points will be established at R.8.c. 8. 6. and R.7.

5. DISTRIBUTION.

RIGHT FRONT Coy. "B"

LEFT FRONT Coy "A"

RIGHT SUPPORT Coy. "D"

LEFT SUPPORT COY. "C"

O/C "C" and "D" Coys will detail two Platoons each as a carrying party. They will carry one tool per man in the proportion of three shovels to one pick.

The 14th H.L.I will detail two Platoons to act as Moppers-up. and who will be responsible for Prisoners &c.

The division between Companies in the Front Line will be

Q 18. d. 2.3 - R 13. a. 8.3 - R.8. C.2.7.

6. DRESS

Fighting Order.

Each man will carry 2 Sand bags

Water bottles to be filled.

O/C. Coys will make the necessary arrangements to draw from forward dumps established at Q.23. b. 8.4 necessary bombs, and to make ammunition up to 220 rounds per man.

7. COMMUNICATIONS.

The main line of Communication will be from Cross Roads Q.23.b.8.3. along the road to VILLERS PLOUICH.

Battalion Headquarters at commencement of operation will be at Q.18.C.8.3 Subsequently in rear of last wave.

8. ZERO TIME.

At Zero hour artillery will put down a barrage as follows.

ZERO.   Barrage on line marked in BLUE.

ZERO. +6 mins.   Barrage will commence to creep forward at the rate of 100 yards in 4 mins. pausing for 10 mins on lines marked in RED.

Barrage will halt and become protective about 200 yards beyond final objectives shown by GREEN lines and continue firing until +120 mins.

9 ASSEMBLY.

Coys will move out on line of Assembly. and be ready by -15 mins.

At ZERO. Coys will move up as close as possible to BARRAGE.

10 FLARES.

The most advanced troops will light 7 flares on being called for by Contact Patrol Aeroplanes.

11. R.A.P.

The R.A.P. will be established at Q 23. C. 8.3.

No 1. 60.
2   OC A
3   B
4   C
5   D
6   14th H.L.)
7   14th A&SH
8   17th Welsh.
9   Odr. off.
10   War Diary.
11   File.
12   Space.

Lieut.

23/4/17   Adjt 13d Bn East Surrey Regiment.

EAST SURREY REGT. O.O. 47.

20/4/17.

REF. 57ᶜ S.E.

1. INTENTION.

The Battalion will capture and occupy the following line on the 21st April, 1917, 15 RAVINE exclusive to Q. 17. d. 8. 7 inclusive, at ZERO TIME + 6 minutes.

2. DISPOSITION.

"D" Coy from 15 Ravine exclusive to the track Q. 18. d. 0. 5.

"C" Coy from Q. 18. c. 7 3 to Q 17. d 8. 7

One Platoon of "A" Coy will be attached to "C" Coy and one Platoon of "A" Coy will be attached to "D" Coy.

"B" Coy will be in SUPPORT at Q. 23. c. 5. 4

Two Platoons of "A" Coy will hold line of Resistance in GOUZEAUCOURT WOOD.

3. REPORTS.

Reports and Messages will be sent to Advanced Bn H.Q. at Q. 23. c. 6. 3 ("C" Coys old H.Q.) which will be in telephonic communication with "C" & "D" Coys.

4. ACTION.

O.C. C & D Coy will push forward Patrols after dark on the night of 20/21st April, and if the objective is unoccupied will at once push forward —

Right Post # to be at least 250 yards from 1⁵ Ravine.

5. FLARES.

O.C. C & D Coys will be responsible that the most advanced Troops will light REDFLARES when called for by Contact aeroplanes.

6. ZERO TIME.

Zero Time will be notified later.

7. T.M.

O.C. 120th T.M.B. will detail one Stokes Mortar to be at Bn H.Q. by 3am and await further orders.

8. PRISONERS.

All prisoners will be sent back to Bn H.Q. immediately.

9. REGIMENTAL AID POST.

Regimental Aid Post will be established at advanced Bn H.Q.

ACKNOWLEDGE.

Issued 11.30 pm
by Runner.

No 1. O.C. A
         B
         C
         D
         T.M.B
    M.O. N/a.
    C.O.
    WAR DIARY
    FILE.

D.Ainslie
Lt Adjt.

EAST SURREY REGT. O.O. 47.

20/4/17.

REF 57ᶜ S.E.

1. INTENTION.

The Battalion will capture and occupy the following line on the 21ˢᵗ April, 1917, 15 RAVINE exclusive to Q.17.d.8.7 inclusive, at ZERO TIME + 6 minutes

2. DISPOSITION.

"D" Coy from 15 Ravine exclusive to the track Q.18.d.0.5.

"C" Coy from Q.18.c.7.3 to Q.17.d.8.7

One Platoon of "A" Coy will be attached to "C" Coy and one Platoon of "A" Coy will be attached to "D" Coy.

"B" Coy will be in SUPPORT at Q.23.c.5.4.

Two Platoons of "A" Coy will hold line of Resistance in GOUZEAUCOURT WOOD.

3. REPORTS.

Reports and Messages will be sent to Advanced Bn H.Q. at Q.23.c.6.3 ("C" Coy's old H.Q.) which will be in telephonic communication with "C" & "D" Coys.

4. ACTION.

O.C. C & D Coys will push forward Patrols after dark on the night of 20/21ˢᵗ April, and if the objective is unoccupied will at once push forward and consolidate.

Right Post to be at least 250 yards from 15 Ravine.

5. FLARES

O.C. C & D Coys will be responsible that the most advanced Troops will light REDFLARES when called for by Contact aeroplanes.

6. ZERO TIME

Zero Time will be notified later.

7. T.M.

O.C. 120th T.M.B. will detail one Stokes Mortar to be at Bn H.Q. by 3am and await further Orders.

8. PRISONERS

All prisoners will be sent back to Bn H.Q. immediately.

9. REGIMENTAL AID POST

Regimental Aid Post will be established at advanced Bn H.Q.

ACKNOWLEDGE.

Issued 11.30 pm
by Runner.

No 1. O.C. A.
      B
      C
      D
      T.M.B
MO. Nho.
10
WAR DIARY
FILE.

Dainsh
Lt. Adjt.

Vol 12

Confidential

War Diary

OF THE

13TH Bn E. East Surrey Regt.

VOLUME. 12

From 1st May 1917. To 31st May 1917:

WAR DIARY

or

~~INTELLIGENCE SUMMARY.~~

(Erase heading not required.)

Army Form C. 2118.

Instructions regarding War Diaries and Intelligence Summaries are contained in F.S. Regs. Part II. and the Staff Manual respectively. Title pages will be prepared in manuscript.

13th Bn East Surrey Regt.
/20th Inf. Bde
40th Division

Place	Date	Hour	Summary of Events and Information	Remarks and references to Appendices
EQUANCOURT	1.5.17		The Battalion relieved the 14th Bn N.Z.I in Brigade support at QUEENS CROSS. Headquarters were established at Q.28 d 30.25	Sketch Refs. 57c S.E. Ex.39 ⅀20000 Y₁M₁Y₁₁
QUEENS CROSS near GOUZEAUCOURT.	4.5.17		Two companies per night worked under the O.C. right Battalion, on the front line.	XMM.W.
	5.5.17		On the night of the 5/6th a raid was made on LANACQUERIE by the 119th, 121st Brigade in conjunction with the 8th Division.	XM.W.
	6.5.17		Lt. Col W.C. NEWTON proceeded to the 15th Corps Rest Station near ABBEVILLE. Major J.H FOSTER 14th N.Z.I took over command of the Battalion. On the night of the 6/7 the Battalion relieved the 14th N.Z.I on the right subsector. Battalion headquarters were established at R.14 a 05.05. The 14th A.I.F were on our right & the 13th Yorks on our left.	XM.W.
VILLERS PLOUICH	7.5.17		During the morning the enemy shelled VILLERS PLOUICH with about 60 4.2s. On the night 7/8th the boundary between the 120th & 121st Inf. Brigades was readjusted. The part of the line to the east of R7 d.5.9 was handed over to the 13th Yorks (121st Brigade)	

2353 Wt. W2544/1454 700,000 5/15 D.D. & L. A.D.S.S./Forms/C. 2118.

Army Form C. 2118.

WAR DIARY

or

~~INTELLIGENCE~~ SUMMARY.

(Erase heading not required.)

13ª Bttn. East Surrey Regt.

Instructions regarding War Diaries and Intelligence
Summaries are contained in F. S. Regs., Part II
and the Staff Manual respectively. Title pages
will be prepared in manuscript.

120ᵗʰ Inf Brigade
40ᵗʰ Division

Place	Date	Hour	Summary of Events and Information	Remarks and references to Appendices
VILLERS PLOUICH	7·5·17		After relief by the 13ᵗʰ Yorks the Battalion redeveloped to the left and occupied a line from R7 d 5.9 to Q12 central. Disposition:- D Cy. right front, C Cy. left front, A Cy. support (intermediate line Q18 a.r.), B Cy. reserve (sunken road Q23 c with 1 platoon in old German trench Q23 & 6.8) Battalion Headquarters Q23 c 6.3.	...
	8·5·17		At 7 p.m. the enemy shelled the intermediate line about Q18c.	...
	9·5·17		Soon after dawn 2 of the enemy were seen walking about in front of our line in Q12 central. They were fired upon by our Lewis guns and killed. A patrol went out and brought in all papers and identifications. The men were found to belong to the 162ⁿᵈ Regt. Between 9 am & 11 am the enemy shelled our trenches at Q12 a & 7 but did no damage. Our artillery were very active the whole day. Capt. CC DOWDING M.C. 11ᵗʰ KORL was temporarily attached to the Battalion as 2nd in Command.	...

2353 Wt. W²⁵⁴¹/¹⁴⁵⁴ 700,000 5/15 D. D. & L. A.D.S.S./Forms/C. 2118.

Army Form C. 2118.

WAR DIARY

or

INTELLIGENCE SUMMARY.

(Erase heading not required.)

13th Battn. East Surrey Regt.

Instructions regarding War Diaries and Intelligence
Summaries are contained in F. S. Regs., Part II.
and the Staff Manual respectively. Title pages
will be prepared in manuscript.

120th Inf. Brigade
40th Division

Place	Date	Hour	Summary of Events and Information	Remarks and references to Appendices
VILLERS PLOUICH	10.5.17	10.30 am	The enemy dropped about 40 4.2's near the intermediate line Q.18c. During the afternoon our artillery shelled the Hindenburg Line. There was considerable aerial activity throughout the day.	M.A.16
	11.5.17		Situation fairly quiet	M.A.6
	12.5.17		The artillery were active on both sides. During the evening the enemy shelled our front line and the sunken road between VILLERS PLOUICH and BEAUCAMP. 2nd Lt W.ANDREW was evacuated to England sick. Casualties 3 O.R. wounded. On the night of the 12th/13th the Battalion was relieved by the 12th K.R.Ris. (60th Inf. Brigade 20th Division). On completion of relief the Battalion moved to billets in SOREL LE GRAND. During this tour the reserve company and two platoons of the support company worked on the front line every night. The fire trenches were deepened. Line steps were made, the wire was considerably thickened and company headquarters for the front line companies were built.	M.A.11

2353 Wt. W2541/1454 700,000 5/15 D. D. & L. A.D.S.S./Forms/C. 2118.

13th Battalion East Surrey Regt.

WAR DIARY

or

INTELLIGENCE SUMMARY.

(Erase heading not required.)

Instructions regarding War Diaries and Intelligence Summaries are contained in F. S. Regs. Part II. and the Staff Manual respectively. Title pages will be prepared in manuscript.

/20th Inf. Brigade
40th Division.

Place	Date	Hour	Summary of Events and Information	Remarks and references to Appendices
SOREL	13/5/17		On the night 13/14th the Battalion relieved the 2nd West Yorks (23rd Inf. Brigade, 8th Division) in Brigade Reserve. Disposition:- C & D Coy. in shelters on the sunken road W6d5.6 to W6b6.0, A & B Coy. in shelters X1c35 to X1c30. Battalion Headquarters W6d6.2.	M.P.O.
St. GOUZEAU COURT	14.5.17		2nd Lt. E.J.J RANDALL reported for duty.	M.P.H.
"	15.5.17		Capt. C.C. DOWDING, M.C. was admitted to Field Ambulance. Capt N.G. WEST 1st Battn. Notts & Derby was appointed 2nd in Command.	M.P.S.
	17.5.17		2nd Lt. L.W. PINNICK reported for duty.	M.P.H.
	18.5.17		On the night 18/19th the Battalion relieved the 14th K.L.I in the right subsector. Disposition:- A Coy. R34d89 to R34a55 D Coy R34a55 to R27a72 B Coy about X2d6.2 ~~B Coy X2d66~~ (with 2 platoons on the Green line about X2c56) C Coy X2d5.81 (with two platoons about X2d97)	M.P.H.

2353 Wt. W2544/1454 700,000 5/15 D. D. & L. A.D.S.S./Forms/C. 2118.

WAR DIARY

or

INTELLIGENCE SUMMARY.

(Erase heading not required.)

13th Battn. East Surrey Regt.

Instructions regarding War Diaries and Intelligence/20th Inf. Brigade
Summaries are contained in F. S. Regs., Part II.
and the Staff Manual respectively. Title pages 40th Division
will be prepared in manuscript.

Place	Date	Hour	Summary of Events and Information	Remarks and references to Appendices
	18.5.17		Whilst in Brigade Reserve the Battalion sent two companies per night for work on the right Battalion front.	W.H.y+
VILLERS GUISLAIN	19.5.17		The enemy shelled R.33 & 6.7 with 77 m.m. but did no damage. 2nd Lt. A.C. THOMPSON was admitted to Field Ambulance sick.	W.H.y+
	20.5.17		Situation quiet. The enemy sent a number of aerial darts and rifle grenades over our front line. The following officers reported for duty. 2nd Lts. C.B. ROSE, H. F. RISKEY, M. MacEWAN, C.F. MOLENKAMP, L.E.M. SAVILL.	W.H.y.
	21.5.17		Our artillery bombarded the enemy's trenches in R.22. Aeroplanes were very active on both sides.	W.H.y+
	22.5.17		Inter company reliefs were carried out. B Coy relieved A Coy. C Coy relieved D Coy. Major J.H. FOSTER rejoined the 14.5.17. Capt. H.G. WEST took over command of the Battalion.	W.H.y+

2353   Wt. W2544/1454 700,000 5/15 D. D. & L.   A.D.S.S./Forms/C. 2118.

WAR DIARY

or

INTELLIGENCE SUMMARY.

(Erase heading not required.)

13th Bn. East Surrey Regt.

20th Inf Brigade
40th Division

Instructions regarding War Diaries and Intelligence Summaries are contained in F. S. Regs., Part II. and the Staff Manual respectively. Title pages will be prepared in manuscript.

Place	Date	Hour	Summary of Events and Information	Remarks and references to Appendices
VILLERS GUISLAIN	23-5-17		On the night 23rd/24th 2nd Lt T.B MILLS went out with a patrol to reconnoitre the enemy wire. The patrol moved its direction and reached the outskirts of BANTEUX R.36.a. 2nd Lt MILLS went forward alone to inspect the wire. The enemy then opened heavy machine gun and rifle fire on the patrol forcing them to withdraw. Search was made for 2nd Lt Mills but he could not be found. The remainder of the patrol returned just as dawn was breaking. 2nd Lts T.E.M. CROWTHER and R.H. ROWLAND reported for duty.	M.H.L.
	24.5.17		The enemy shelled the left Company Headquarters and the neighbouring heavy trench mortar emplacement (R.33.b.5.8) but did no damage.	M.H.L.
	25.5.17		The Battalion were relieved by the 17th Bn Lancs Fusiliers (35th Division) and withdrew via GOUZEAUCOURT to DESSART WOOD where accommodation was provided in tents and shelters.	M.H.L.

2353 Wt. W²⁵⁴⁴/1454 700,000 5/15 D. D. & L.   A.D.S.S./Forms/C. 2118.

WAR DIARY

or

INTELLIGENCE SUMMARY.

(Erase heading not required.)

13ᵗʰ Battn. East Surrey Regt.

Instructions regarding War Diaries and Intelligence/20ᵗʰ Inf. Brigade
Summaries are contained in F. S. Regs., Part II.   40ᵗʰ Division.
and the Staff Manual respectively.   Title pages
will be prepared in manuscript.

Place	Date	Hour	Summary of Events and Information	Remarks and references to Appendices
DESSART WOOD	26.5.17		Brigadier-General the Hon C.S.W DRUMMOND WILLOUGHBY C.M.G. presented Military Medal ribbons to No 10352 Corpl W MORGAN, and No 17409 Corpl G.K. JENNINGS. On the night 26/27ᵗʰ the Battalion relived the 11ᵗʰ K.O.R.L Regt in Brigade support in position ABC+D Companies in the Green Line about R31 central Battn Headquarters in the Quarry R31 c 7.8.	M/lru
GOUZEAUCOURT	27.5.17		During the night 27/28 A Coy moved forward and occupied the Reserve Trench. R 26 central) B.C+D Companies redeveloped to the left and a Company of the 14ᵗʰ A.R.L.I occupied the right Company position in the Green Line D Coy worked in the reserve line building shelters on the right of A Coy. B"C Coy¹ sapped out from the front line of the left Battalion	M/lru
	28/5.17 30		Under cover of darkness BC+D Coy carried on as on the 27ᵗʰ A Coy built shelters in the Reserve line. On the morning of the 30ᵗʰ a chance shell fell on the Green Line about R31 central. Casualties 3 oR Killed 2 oR wounded	M/lru

2353 Wt. W2544/1454 700,000 5/15 D. D. & L.   A.D.S.S./Forms/C. 2118.

WAR DIARY

or

INTELLIGENCE SUMMARY.

(Erase heading not required.)

13ᵗʰ Battⁿ East Surrey Regt.

Instructions regarding War Diaries and Intelligence
Summaries are contained in F. S. Regs. Part II.
and the Staff Manual respectively. Title pages
will be prepared in manuscript.

120ᵗʰ Inf Brigade
40ᵗʰ Division

Place	Date	Hour	Summary of Events and Information	Remarks and references to Appendices
GOUZEAUCOURT	31.5.17		Lt. Col. W.C. NEWTON returned from the Corps Rest Station	
			Sir D. Haig's of 9ᵗʰ April 1917. (Supplement to the London Gazette of May 22ⁿᵈ) The following Officers + others were "Mentioned in Despatches" vide the Times dated 23.5.17 Lt. Col. W.C. NEWTON Lt + Capt. F. SAINGER Hon. Lt. + Q.M. F. FOSTER Nᵒ 13015 Sergt. G HOLMES.	WₜNₜₛ

W. Newton
Lieut. Col.
Cmdg 13ᵗʰ Bⁿ East Surrey Regiment.

War Diary

OF THE

13ᵀᴴ Bⁿ. Eᵈ. East Surrey Regt.

VOLUME. 14

From 1ˢᵗ June 1917. To 30ᵏ June 1917.

Confidential

13th Bn. East Surrey Regt.

Army Form C. 2118.

WAR DIARY
or
INTELLIGENCE SUMMARY.
(Erase heading not required.)

Instructions regarding War Diaries and Intelligence
Summaries are contained in F. S. Regs., Part II.
and the Staff Manual respectively. Title pages
will be prepared in manuscript.

1/20th Inf. Bde.
40th Division

Place	Date	Hour	Summary of Events and Information	Remarks and references to Appendices
GOUZEAUCOURT	1.6.17		The Battalion remained in Brigade Support. Bn.H.Q. were in the Quarry R.31.c.8.8	Map Ref. 57c S.E. Edition 4a. 1/20000. Bn.H.Q.
	2.6.17		2nd Lt. E.J.J. RANDALL proceeded to England to join the Royal Engineers School, Newark. The 40th Division became part of the 3rd Corps.	Bn.H.Q.
	3.6.17		On the night 3/4th the Battalion relieved the 14th Bn. H.L.I. in the left subsector right section. GONNELIEU. Disposition A Cy. (+ 1 platoon C Cy.) on the right B Cy on the left D Cy in support and C Cy (less one platoon) in Reserve. Battn. Hqrs. were established in the Quarry R.25.a.3.9.	Bn.H.Q.
GONNELIEU SECTOR.	4.6.17		Situation fairly quiet. Machine guns active on both sides.	Bn.H.Q.
	5.6.17		The enemy shelled Battalion Headquarters but did no damage. Our artillery retaliated on enemy front line.	Bn.H.Q.

2353 Wt. W2541/1454 700,000 5/15 D. D. & L. A.D.S.S./Forms/C. 2118.

WAR DIARY

or

INTELLIGENCE SUMMARY.

(Erase heading not required.)

13th Bn. East Surrey Regt.

Instructions regarding War Diaries and Intelligence 120th Inf Bde
Summaries are contained in F. S. Regs., Part II.
and the Staff Manual respectively. Title pages   40th Division
will be prepared in manuscript.

Place	Date	Hour	Summary of Events and Information	Remarks and references to Appendices
GONNELIEU SECTOR.	6.6.17		During the day our artillery shelled enemy's front line and communication trenches.	M.H.B.
	7.6.17		Situation quiet. On the night 7/8th C Cy relieved A Cy and D Cy relieved B Cy.	M.H.B.
	8.6.17		Occasional interchange of shells by the enemy and our artillery.	M.H.B.
	9.6.17		A fighting patrol went out from our lines about midnight with the object of capturing an enemy patrol. It remained out about an hour to half without seeing any signs of the enemy.	M.H.B.
	10.6.17		Enemy machine guns were very active throughout the night.	M.H.B.
	11.6.17		The 121st Bde relieved the 120th Bde on the night 11/12th. The Battalion was relieved by the 20th Bn Middlesex Regt. On completion	M.H.B.

2353 Wt. W2541/1454 700,000 5/15 D. D. & L. A.D.S.S./Forms/C. 2118.

13th. Bn. East Surrey Regt.

WAR DIARY

or

INTELLIGENCE SUMMARY.

(Erase heading not required.)

Instructions regarding War Diaries and Intelligence 120th Inf. Bde.
Summaries are contained in F. S. Regs., Part II.
and the Staff Manual respectively. Title pages   40th Division
will be prepared in manuscript.

Place	Date	Hour	Summary of Events and Information	Remarks and references to Appendices
GONNELIEU SECTOR	11.6.17		Relief the Battalion withdrew to DESSART Wd when accommodation was provided in tents and shelters. Route - QUARRY (R31 c 87) FINS-GOUZEAUCOURT Road.	M.H.L.
DESSART WOOD	12.6.17 to 15.6.17		Platoon and Company training according to the Battalion Programme of work. Lieut. J.R.HUCKER was appointed Assistant Adjutant.	M.H.L.
	16.6.17		Brigadier-General Hon. C.S.H.DRUMMOND-WILLOUGHBY C.M.G. presented Corpl. H.R.NAUNTON with D.S.O. ribband. A representative of the French Mission presented No 13290 Corpl. E.FOSTER with MEDAILLE MILITAIRE ribband	M.H.L.
	17.6.17		Battalion sports were held.	M.H.L.
	18/19. 6.17		All available men were employed on working parties.	M.H.L.

2353. Wt. W2544/1454 700,000 5/15 D. D. & L.   A.D.S.S./Forms/C. 2118.

Army Form C. 2118.

WAR DIARY

or

INTELLIGENCE-SUMMARY.

(*Erase heading not required.*)

13th Bn East Surrey Regt.

Instructions regarding War Diaries and Intelligence Summaries are contained in F. S. Regs. Part II. and the Staff Manual respectively. Title pages will be prepared in manuscript.

Place	Date	Hour	Summary of Events and Information	Remarks and references to Appendices
DESSART WOOD	19.6.17		The 120th Inf. Bde relieved the 119th Inf. Bde in the VILLERS PLOUICH Sector. The Battn. relieved the 12th Bn. SWB. in Brigade Reserve. Btattgs. were established at Q 29 b 2.0.	Mt.
VILLERS PLOUICH SECTOR.	20/27 6.17		Whilst in Bde Reserve large parties were sent up nightly for work on the front line of the right front Battalion. On the 22nd Lt. Col. W.E. NEWTON presented the D.C.M. ribband to No. 11123 I/Cpl. J.W. REED. Casualties. Capt. H.P. NAUNTON D.S.O. and 2 o.r. wounded 24th. 2nd Lt. A.C. THOMPSON returned from hospital 25th. Capt. F.J.T. HANN was evacuated sick to CCS 26th. On the night 27/28th the Battalion relieved the 11th Bn. KORL Regt. in the right sub sector. Disposition.— A Cy on the right. B Cy on the left. C " in support. D " in reserve	Mt.

2353 Wt. W3441/1451 700,000 5/15 D. D. & L. A.D.S.S./Forms/C. 2118.

13th Bn East Surrey Regt.

WAR DIARY

or

INTELLIGENCE SUMMARY.

(Erase heading not required.)

Instructions regarding War Diaries and Intelligence 1/20th Inf Bde.
Summaries are contained in F. S. Regs., Part II. 40th Division
and the Staff Manual respectively. Title pages
will be prepared in manuscript.

Place	Date	Hour	Summary of Events and Information	Remarks and references to Appendices
VILLERS PLOUICH SECTOR			Two platoons were sent out as covering Parties to guard our front during the relief. These parties remained out until 2 a.m. without having seen any of the enemy.	M.H.
	28.5.17		A fighting Patrol left our lines at R.14.d.9.7 and advanced to the enemy's wire without encountering any enemy Patrols. The enemy shelled R.14.d.5.8 but did little damage. Casualties 2 o.r. killed 2 o.r. wounded.	
	29.5.17		Lt. Col. HG NEWTON proceeded to England on leave (1-11 July) Major WG WEST took over command of the Battalion. At midnight 29/30 the enemy sent up a green rocket and immediately opened a heavy barrage on our right front and support trenches. At the same time the enemy attempted to raid our enemy about R.15.c.0.7. The raiding party were however noticed by one of our sentries and Lewis gun and rifle fire was immediately opened. Evidently surprised	M.H.

2353 Wt. W2544/1454 700,000 5/15 D. D. & L. A.D.S.S./Forms/C. 2118.

Army Form C. 2118.

WAR DIARY
or
INTELLIGENCE SUMMARY.

(*Erase heading not required.*)

Instructions regarding War Diaries and Intelligence
Summaries are contained in F. S. Regs., Part II.
and the Staff Manual respectively. Title pages
will be prepared in manuscript.

13ᵗʰ Bn. East Surrey Regt.

20 ᵗʰ Inf. Bde.

40 ᵗʰ Division

Place	Date	Hour	Summary of Events and Information	Remarks and references to Appendices
VILLERS PLOUICH SECTOR.	29.6.17		By this reception the enemy threw bombs before reaching bombing distance and did no damage. The enemy were completely repulsed. Sounds of men groaning from the direction of the enemy indicate that some were hit by our fire. The strength of the party was estimated to have been between 20 + 30 men.	
			At 12.30 a.m. the enemy sent up 2 signals each bursting into 3 golden balls. The enemy artillery then ceased fire. Our artillery retaliated on the enemy front trenches. Casualties. 8 o.r. slightly wounded.	Pℋℛ L
	30.6.17		During the day our snipers were very active and claimed several hits. At internal throughout the night the enemy used a searchlight which appeared to be in his front line about R.15 c 2.4. This light showed up all our working and covering parties.	
			No. 13290 Corpl E. FOSTER was awarded the VICTORIA CROSS for	

2353 Wt. W 2544/1454 500,000 5/15 D. D. & L. A.D.S.S./Forms/C. 2118.

13ᵗʰ Bn. East Surrey Regt.

WAR DIARY

or

INTELLIGENCE SUMMARY.

(Erase heading not required.)

Instructions regarding War Diaries and Intelligence /20ᵗʰ Inf Bde.
Summaries are contained in F. S. Regs. Part II.   40ᵗʰ Division
and the Staff Manual respectively. Title pages
will be prepared in manuscript.

Place	Date	Hour	Summary of Events and Information	Remarks and references to Appendices
	30·6·17		conspicuous bravery and initiative in the attack on VILLERS PLOUICH "24ᵗʰ April 1917."	M.H.L.
			Notification was received that Lieut C J NOAKES was struck off the establishment of the Battalion as from 5·4·17	

M.H.Lucker Lieut   for Major

Comdg 13ᵗʰ Bn East Surrey Regt.

Vol 14

M.O.

14.D.
14 sheets

War Diary

of the

13th Bn. D. East Surrey Regt.

VOLUME. 14

From 1st July 1917. To 31st July 1917.

13ᵗʰ Battn. East Surrey Regt.

WAR DIARY

or

INTELLIGENCE SUMMARY.

(Erase heading not required.)

Instructions regarding War Diaries and Intelligence
Summaries are contained in F. S. Regs., Part II.
and the Staff Manual respectively. Title pages
will be prepared in manuscript.

190ᵗʰ Inf. Bde.
40ᵗʰ Division.

Place	Date	Hour	Summary of Events and Information	Remarks and references to Appendices
VILLERS PLOUICH SECTOR	1.7.17		Our artillery were fairly quiet throughout the day. Enemy trench mortars and artillery fired on saphead R15 c 0.7 causing slight casualties. Patrols of 1 officer & 12 o.r. and 1 officer & 30 o.r. with Lewis gun searched No Man's Land but saw no enemy patrols or parties. Two bodies of dead Boches were found outside our wire at R15 c 0.7 and a large number of bombs were seen at intervals towards enemy's saphead R15 c 55.35 (emanuil road 29ᵗʰ dft) Enemy searchlights about R9 central and LAVACQUERIE were very active. Inter Company reliefs were carried out. C Cʸ relieved A Cʸ in right front & D Cʸ relieved B Cʸ in left front. Lt Colonel W.C.NEWTON proceed to England on short leave. 2ⁿᵈ Lieut G.S.DREN was evacuated to England (sick) 19.6.17. Casualties 1 o.r killed. 1 o.r wounded.	Map ref. 57ᴰ S.E. 1/20,000 Ed. 4.A.

W.H.T. |
| | 2.7.17 | | During the morning enemy trench mortars fired at intervals along the left Company front. At night our patrols were out as usual but saw no signs of the enemy. | |

2353 Wt. W 2541/1454 700,000 5/15 D. D. & L. A.D.S.S./Forms/C. 2118.

13th Battalion East Surrey Regt.

WAR DIARY
or
INTELLIGENCE SUMMARY.

(Erase heading not required.)

Instructions regarding War Diaries and Intelligence
Summaries are contained in F. S. Regs., Part II.
and the Staff Manual respectively. Title pages
will be prepared in manuscript.

/20th Inf. Brigade
40th Division

Place	Date	Hour	Summary of Events and Information	Remarks and references to Appendices
	2.7.17		Lieut. A.B. BURTON and Lieut. W.N LOWE. 14th M.G.S. were attached for duty.	Initials
	3.7.17		Our snipers were very active and claimed several hits on enemy walking along sky line about R.15.d. Patrols maintained touch with flank Battalions and encountered none of the enemy. Chain of golden lights and green rockets were sent up from LAVACQUERIE by the enemy but no apparent action followed. The Brigade frontage was rearranged. The Right Cy took over from 19th D.W.R. up to R.20.b.65. The Left Cy handed over to 14th A.& S.H. up to ARGYLL SAP (exclusive) R.14.b.77. Company fronts now as follows: Right. R.20.b.65. to R.14.d.85.75 inclusive of Sap & T.Head. Left. R.14.d.88 to Sap R.14.b.45.60 – R.14.b.70.70. Lt. Colonel E.C. ATKINS 2/5 Leicester Regt. rejoined from Senior Officers Course. 2nd Lt. R.W.H. KING admitted to Fd. Ambulance.	Initials

2353   Wt. W2541/1454   700,000   5/15   D. D. & L.   A.D.S.S./Forms/C. 2118.

13ᵗʰ Battn. East Surrey Regt.

WAR DIARY

or

~~INTELLIGENCE SUMMARY.~~

(Erase heading not required.)

120ᵗʰ Inf. Brigade
40ᵗʰ Division.

Instructions regarding War Diaries and Intelligence
Summaries are contained in F. S. Regs., Part II.
and the Staff Manual respectively. Title pages
will be prepared in manuscript.

Place	Date	Hour	Summary of Events and Information	Remarks and references to Appendices
	4.7.17		Both our and the enemy artillery were very active throughout the day. Our patrols searched No mans land as usual. Casualties 3 o.r wounded.	W.H.E.
	5.7.17		About 1.30 a.m. the enemy heavily shelled right Company front causing several casualties. Our artillery retaliated on the enemy front line. Casualties 2nd Lt. M.MCEWAN and 1 o.r killed. 10 o.r wounded. On the night of 5/6 the Battalion was relieved by 11ᵗʰ Bn. K.O.R.L. and withdrew to Brigade Support in 15 Ravine with A Coy in the GOUZEAUCOURT - TRESCAULT Road Q.30 L.	W.H.E.
15. RAVINE.	6.7.17		Two Companies worked on the right Battalion front during the night. 2nd Lt. R.H. ROWLAND was admitted to Field Ambulance.	W.H.E.

2353 Wt. W₃541/1454 700,000 5/15 D. D. & L. A.D.S.S./Forms/C. 2118.

Army Form C. 2118.

WAR DIARY

or

INTELLIGENCE SUMMARY.

(Erase heading not required.)

13ᵗʰ Battn. East Surrey Regt.
20ᵗʰ Inf. Brigade
40ᵗʰ Division.

Instructions regarding War Diaries and Intelligence Summaries are contained in F.S. Regs., Part II. and the Staff Manual respectively. Title pages will be prepared in manuscript.

Place	Date	Hour	Summary of Events and Information	Remarks and references to Appendices
	7.7.17		At night one Company worked on right Battalion front. Casualties 1 o.r. wounded.	M⁴₂
	8.7.17		Several new shelters were completed and a new Aid Post started in 1ˢᵗ Ravine. One Company worked on right Battalion front as usual. Casualties:- 1 o.r killed (accidentally) 1 o.r. wounded.	M⁴₂
	9.7.17		Considerable improvement was made to the area occupied by the Battalion. About 11 p.m. enemy shelled 1ˢᵗ Ravine but did no damage. At night one Company worked on new front line. Capt. H.R. NAUNTON DSO was evacuated to England.	M⁴₂
	10.7.17		Work on shelters and Regt. Aid Post continued. One Company worked on front line as usual.	M⁴₂

2353 Wt. W2544/1454 700,000 5/15 D.D.&L. A.D.S.S./Forms/C. 2118.

13th Battn. East Surrey Regt.

120th Inf. Brigade

40th Division.

WAR DIARY
or
INTELLIGENCE SUMMARY.

(Erase heading not required.)

Instructions regarding War Diaries and Intelligence
Summaries are contained in F. S. Regs., Part II.
and the Staff Manual respectively. Title pages
will be prepared in manuscript.

Place	Date	Hour	Summary of Events and Information	Remarks and references to Appendices
	11.7.17		Work as for previous day.	
			Hon. Lt. & Qr. Mr. J. Foster admitted to Field Ambulance (gas). 1 or wounded.	M.Hr.
	12.7.17		Lt. Colonel W.C. NEWTON returned from leave.	
			Casualties 1 or. wounded.	M.Hr.
	13.7.17		On the night 13/14 the Battalion relieved the 11th KORL in the right subsector VILLERS PLOUICH sector.	
			Disposition:- Bn. HQ in Quarry R.20.a.2.9. D Cy. on right, C Cy. on left B Cy. in support & A Cy. in Reserve.	
			Battalion frontage extended from R.20 to 8.6.6 & R.14 b.9.8.	
			On our right was 19th Bn. S.W.B. & on our left was 14th Bn. A.& S.H.	
			Casualties 1 or. wounded.	M.Hr.
MILLERS PLOUICH SECTOR	14.7.17		Enemy shelled POPE AVENUE & NEWPORT TRENCH (R.14 d.7.7) intermittently throughout the day.	M.Hr.
			Casualties 2 or. killed 7 or. wounded.	

2353 Wt. W2541/1454 700,000 5/15 D.D.&L.   A.D.S.S./Forms/C. 2118.

WAR DIARY

or

~~INTELLIGENCE SUMMARY.~~

(Erase heading not required.)

13th Battn. East Surrey Regt.
/20th Inf. Bde
40th Division.

Instructions regarding War Diaries and Intelligence
Summaries are contained in F. S. Regs., Part II.
and the Staff Manual respectively. Title pages
will be prepared in manuscript.

Place	Date	Hour	Summary of Events and Information	Remarks and references to Appendices
	15.7.17		About 5.15 p.m. our artillery put a concentrated bombardment on PINE COPSE (R.8.a).	
			Between 10 p.m. and 10.30 p.m. the enemy shelled POPE AVENUE. Very lights were fired very often. Our patrols found the enemy very alert.	M.F.
			Frequently the enemy bombed his own front frequently & at short intervals. Casualties: 2 o.r. wounded.	
	16.7.17		Between 8 a.m. & 9 a.m. enemy fired 15 4.2s + 77 m.ms. on new front line at R.14.a.9.4 apparently registering. POPE AVENUE was shelled between 10 p.m. & 11.30 p.m. about R.14.a.2.8 & R.14.a.2.0	M.F.
			Capt. F.J.T. HANN was evacuated to England.	
			2nd Lt. L.F. MENZIES-JONES was admitted to F.Amb" (sick)	
	17.7.17		At 5.30 p.m. enemy fired 6 rifle grenades at our left Company front.	
			2nd Lt. L.I. DEACON rejoined the Battalion.	
			On the night 17/18 inter Company reliefs were carried out ...	

2353 Wt. W2544/1454 700,000 5/15 D. D. & L.   A.D.S.S./Forms/C. 2118.

13ᵗʰ Battalion East Surrey Regt. **WAR DIARY**

120ᵗʰ Inf. Brigade. *or*

40ᵗʰ Division. **INTELLIGENCE SUMMARY.**

(Erase heading not required.)

Instructions regarding War Diaries and Intelligence
Summaries are contained in F. S. Regs., Part II.
and the Staff Manual respectively. Title pages
will be prepared in manuscript.

Place	Date	Hour	Summary of Events and Information	Remarks and references to Appendices
	17.7.17	ctd.	A Cy relieved D Cy on the right; B Cy relieved C Cy on the left. Casualties 1 o.r. killed 2 o.r. wounded.	M⁴Ts.
	18.7.17		Our artillery bombarded LA VACQUERIE at 11.30 a.m. The enemy retaliated with about 6 5.9s on NEWPORT TRENCH in the vicinity of R.14 b.5.6. Patrols searched Nomans Land but encountered none of the enemy.	M⁴Ts.
	19.7.17		Our snipers were very active during the day, claiming several hits. A patrol examined the enemy's wire about R.9.c.0.0. and found it about 20 feet thick and 5 feet high.	M⁴Ts.
	20.7.17		About 3.15 a.m. the enemy dropped 14 medium trench mortar shells on NEWPORT TRENCH (R.14 b & 8.3). Our artillery retaliated with 30 18 pounders on the enemy front line. On the night 20/21 two raids on the enemy's lines were attempted. Casualties 2ⁿᵈ Lieut A.L. ANDERSON + 3 o.r. wounded. Reports are given in Appendix I.	M⁴Ts.

2353 Wt. W2341/1454 700,000 5/15 D. D. & L. A.D.S.S./Forms/C. 2118.

Army Form C. 2118.

WAR DIARY

or

~~INTELLIGENCE SUMMARY.~~

(Erase heading not required.)

13th Battalion East Surrey Regt.

Intelligence 120th Inf. Brigade, Part II.

40th Division.

Instructions regarding War Diaries and Intelligence Summaries are contained in F. S. Regs., Part II. and the Staff Manual respectively. Title pages will be prepared in manuscript.

Place	Date	Hour	Summary of Events and Information	Remarks and references to Appendices
	9/7/17		During the morning the enemy bombarded NEWPORT TRENCH between FUSILIER TRENCH and FORE AVENUE. No. 13890 Corpl. E. FOSTER was presented with the Victoria Cross by H. M. the King. On the night 21/22 the Battalion was relieved by the 14th H.L.I. and moved into Brigade Reserve. Disposition: Bn. JHQ. + C Cy. in the GOUZEAUCOURT - TRESCAULT Road Q 30 d 8.8.; A Cy. in the Sunken road Q 29 d 1.8 ; B Cy. in Sunken road Q 29 a 9.4 ; D Cy. in camp South of DESSART WOOD. 2nd Lt. E.C. ATKINS was granted Special leave to England.	M.H.
GOUZEAUCOURT.	23/28.7.17		During this period each Company spent 2 days in the camp near DESSART WOOD obtaining baths + firing on the range. Two companies worked on the left Battalion front each night. Casualties - 26th: 3 o.r. killed 7 o.r. wounded 28th 1 o.r. wounded.	M.H.

2353 Wt. W2544/1454 700,000 5/15 D. D. & L.   A.D.S.S./Forms/C. 2118.

WAR DIARY
or
INTELLIGENCE SUMMARY.

(Erase heading not required.)

Instructions regarding War Diaries and Intelligence Summaries are contained in F. S. Regs., Part II. and the Staff Manual respectively. Title pages will be prepared in manuscript.

120th Inf. Brigade. 40th Division.

Place	Date	Hour	Summary of Events and Information	Remarks and references to Appendices
	29.7.17		2nd Lts. F.G. WHEATCROFT and F.T. CHITTY reported for duty. On the night 29/30 the Battalion relieved the 11th K.O.R.L. in the left subsector. VILLERS PLOUICH section. Disposition; Bn. HQ sunken road R.23.a.9.9. D Cy right front, C Cy left front, A Cy right support, B Cy left support. The Battalion front extended from R.14.b.5.7 to R.7 & 9.1. On our right was 14th Bn. A.I.F. on left 173rd Inf. Bde.	MM.
	30.7.17		Between 6 pm & 7 pm the enemy shelled MERTHYR TRENCH at R.7 & 8.5.95 with about 50 rounds 4.2s & 77s.	MM.
	31.7.17		2nd Lieut. W.G. RRICE reported for duty. Casualties 1 or. killed 1 or. wounded.	MM.
			The following promotions appeared in the London Gazette date 12.7.17 & 18.7.17. T/Lieut & Adjt. E.S. AINGER to be T/Capt. Regt. (22.2.17) T/Lieut F.T.T. HANN to be T/Capt. (25.4.17) T/2 Lieut A.L. ANDERSON to be T/Lieut (25.4.17) T/2 Lieut J.R. HUCKER to be T/Lieut (25.4.17)	

W. Martin
Lt. Colonel
Cmdg. 13th Bn East Surrey Regt.

A 584 Wt. W4973 M687 750,000 750,000 8/16 D.D. & L. Ltd. Forms/C.2118/13.

Bn. East Surrey Rgt

WAR DIARY

or

INTELLIGENCE SUMMARY.

(Erase heading not required.)

Instructions regarding War Diaries and Intelligence
Summaries are contained in F. S. Regs., Part II.
and the Staff Manual respectively. Title pages
will be prepared in manuscript.

Place	Date	Hour	Summary of Events and Information	Remarks and references to Appendices
APPENDIX I			REPORT. ON MINOR ENTERPRISE N°1 ON THE NIGHT 20/21st JULY 1917.	

A patrol consisting of 2nd Lt J. W. Wilson and 20 other ranks with a Lewis Gun left our lines at
ARGYLL SAP (R.14. b. 71/) at 11 p.m. with the object of bringing in a German notice board situated in
the enemy's lines at R.15 a. 5b 65.

The patrol proceeded on a true bearing of 91° and by careful crawling reached the belt of wire surrounding
the objective without having been observed. As soon as they started to cut the wire a small hand searchlight
played on the board and 2 machine guns opened a cross fire on the party wounding 2 men.

The patrol withdrew some 30 yards and the two wounded men, refusing assistance from the party
crawled back to our lines independently.   When the machine gun fire ceased the party
crawled forward to within 10 yards of the wire. 2nd Lt Wilson with 2 other ranks then advanced
and again commenced to cut the wire. Exactly the same results followed - the searchlight
and the machine guns played on the board under the party. 2nd Lt Wilson withdrew the patrol
and waited one hour in No man's Land.   He then advanced a third time and attempted
to reach the board. Orders in German were distinctly heard in the trench ahead and
immediately heavy rifle and machine gun fire was opened on the party who were forced to lie
perfectly still for some 10 minutes. Realising that any further attempt to obtain the
board would meet with similar opposition, he carefully withdrew his patrol retaining no further
casualties

2353 Wt. W°3544/1454 700,000 5/15. D. D. & L.   A.D.S.S./Forms/C. 2118.

Army Form C. 2118.

WAR DIARY

or

INTELLIGENCE SUMMARY.

(Erase heading not required.)

Instructions regarding War Diaries and Intelligence
Summaries are contained in F. S. Regs., Part II.
and the Staff Manual respectively. Title pages
will be prepared in manuscript.

Place	Date	Hour	Summary of Events and Information	Remarks and references to Appendices
			2nd Lt Wilson reports that the wire around the bund is about 2 feet thick and 3 feet high. The dimensions of the bund are approximately 7'×4' and it appeared to look very solid and heavy. The artillery cooperated with occasional shots on points where suspected machine guns and searchlights were placed but as most of the shells were "duds" their fire had no effect.	
			REPORT ON MINOR ENTERPRISE No 2 ON THE NIGHT 20/21st JULY 1917.	
			A party consisting of Lieut Scott. Lieut Anderson and 30 other ranks left ARGYLL SAP. R14.8.77 at 10.45 p.m. with the object of entering the enemy trench at R q c.1.1. (with the help of a bangalore torpedo) to secure identifications and to do as much damage as possible. They were divided into two groups (1) the torpedo party of 15 O.Rs under Lt Scott and (2) the raiding party of 15 O.Rs under Lt Anderson. Of the first group 8 men were used to carry the torpedo and the remainder formed a covering party. The whole party proceeded without interruption to within 80 yards of the enemy wire when a slight noise attracted Lt Scotts attention. This was immediately followed by bombs bursting about 10 yards in front of the covering party. About 35 to 40 of the enemy then rushed towards our covering party who opened rapid fire and threw bombs, holding up the enemy and forcing them to lie down. Lt Anderson and his party, who were about 50 yards in rear then came forward to reinforce the covering party. Lt Scott ordered the men carrying the torpedo to withdraw it to safety and the	

2353 Wt W2544/1454 700,000 5/15 D. D. & L.   A.D.S.S./Forms/C. 2118.

WAR DIARY

or

INTELLIGENCE SUMMARY.

(Erase heading not required.)

13th Bn East Surrey Regt

Instructions regarding War Diaries and Intelligence
Summaries are contained in F. S. Regs., Part II.
and the Staff Manual respectively. Title pages
will be prepared in manuscript.

Place	Date	Hour	Summary of Events and Information	Remarks and references to Appendices
			remaining 22 men under Lts Scott and Anderson rushed forward to within 15 yards of the wire in pursuit of the enemy who hurriedly withdrew to their trenches. Our party was then subjected to very heavy machine gun fire which checked any further advance. At this point Lt Anderson was wounded and great difficulty was experienced in bringing him in to our lines. No enemy wounded could be seen although groans had been heard after our first burst of fire. When the machine gun fire quietened down, Lt Scott carefully withdrew the party sustaining no further casualties. The tapes used as guide lines and the bangalore torpedo were brought back safely to our trenches.	

W. Hunter Lt Col

Comd.g 13th East Surrey Regt.

2333   Wt. W2541/1454 700,000 5/15 D. D. & L.   A.D.S.S./Forms/C. 2118.

War Diary.

of the

13th Bn. East Surrey Regt.

VOLUME 16

From Aug: 1st 1917. to Aug: 31st 1917.

13th BATTALION
EAST SURREY REGIMENT

WAR DIARY
or
INTELLIGENCE SUMMARY.

(Erase heading not required.)

Army Form C. 2118.

Instructions regarding War Diaries and Intelligence
Summaries are contained in F. S. Regs. Part II, and
the Staff Manual respectively. Title pages will be
prepared in manuscript.

123rd INF. BRIGADE
40th DIVISION.

Place	Date	Hour	Summary of Events and Information	Remarks and references to Appendices
VILLERS PLOUICH	1.8.17.		Patrol of 1 Officer and 8 o.R. and 2 o.R. left our lines at R.8.d.33 and R.7.d.90.95. Enemy was very quiet. No hostile patrols were encountered. Our artillery fired 12 rounds on FARM TRENCH at R.8.d.68. Enemy nearly working on parapet in FARM TRENCH R.d.a.5.6. fired at. any believed hit. Enemy light T.M. fired 12 rounds into SURREY RAVINE. No damage was done.	[initials]
	2.8.17.		Readjustment of Corps Front. Ing. Vest R.H. Portland classified as wounded (shell shock). Artry D.A.B.C.69th dated 1/6/17). (Adamthy Field Ambulance 6/7/17). Patrol of 1 Officer and 12 o.R. left our lines at R.8.d.33. No sign of enemy. Patrol was fired on by enemy Machine gun from FARM TRENCH. Artillery quiet. 16 rounds. H.E. Unified fired on Railway at R.8.6.04 at 4.30 p.m. Four enemy were observed working on track of SUNKEN ROAD R.d.6.93. When fired on. One man was seen to fall, and party disappeared. At 11.45 a.m. Enemy shelled MERTHYR TRENCH about 20 rounds 142 and 77 m.m.	[initials]
	3.8.17.		Patrol of 1 Officer and 10 O.R. and 1 Officer and 12 O.R. left our line at R.8.d.33. and R.7.6.5.1. No Man's Land was searched. No enemy patrol was encountered. Enemy was working heavily in FARM TRENCH at R.8.d.5.6. After pigeon-toes shewed Enemy Medley SURREY RAVINE with 12 round 77 m.m. 10.30 a.m. 1045 p.m. Our artillery fired about 60 rounds in vicinity of PINE COPSE.	[initials]

A5834 Wt. W4973 M687 750,000 8/16 D. D. & L. Ltd. Forms/C.2118/13.

WAR DIARY

or

INTELLIGENCE SUMMARY.

(Erase heading not required.)

13th BATTALION
EAST SURREY REGIMENT.

120th BRIGADE
40th DIVISION

Instructions regarding War Diaries and Intelligence
Summaries are contained in F. S. Regs., Part II.
and the Staff Manual respectively. Title pages
will be prepared in manuscript.

Place	Date	Hour	Summary of Events and Information	Remarks and references to Appendices
	4.8.17.		Patrol of 1 Officer and 10 O.R. and 2 Officers and 7 O.R. left our line at R.8.d.3.3. and R.7.6.8.1. and reached the wire. Battalion front. No enemy patrols were encountered. Sounds of working again heard in FARM TRENCH. Our artillery was firing throughout the day, then working on parapet in FARM TRENCH at R.8.6.00. fired at but not believed hit. Enemy artillery fired 4.2's & 4.2 in SORREY RAVINE damage slight.	[initials]
	5.8.17.		Lt.Col. E.C. Atkins left for England. Much movement on the line Ridge in N.5.b. In FARM TRENCH taught working party Ht. Claimed at R.8.a.6.2. Patrols of 1 Officer and 10 O.R. and 1 Officer and 7 O.R. left our line at R.8.d.3.3. and R.7.6.8.1. Moon very bright. Patrol operation debarred to machine gun fire. Enemy was very quiet.	[initials]
	6.8.17.		On the afternoon 1st Battalion was relieved by the 14th A. & S.H. 2nd Lieut. E.M. Dobb joined the Battalion.	[initials]
	7.8.17.		Parades made. Company manoeuvres.	[initials]

A5834 Wt. W4973 M687. 750,000 8/16 D. D. & L. Ltd. Forms/C.2118/13.

Army Form C. 2118.

WAR DIARY

or

INTELLIGENCE SUMMARY.

(Erase heading not required.)

13th BATTALION
EAST SURREY REGIMENT / 120th BRIGADE
40th Division

Instructions regarding War Diaries and Intelligence Summaries are contained in F. S. Regs., Part II. and the Staff Manual respectively. Title pages will be prepared in manuscript.

Place	Date	Hour	Summary of Events and Information	Remarks and references to Appendices
	8.8.17		Parades such. Company arrangements. In the afternoon the G.O.C. presented the riband of the Military Cross to 2/Lieut. J. Wilson.	
	9.8.17		Platoon and Company inspection and training according to Battalion programme. 2/Lieut. R.W. King returned from hospital.	
	10.8.17		Parades such. Company arrangements. In the afternoon the Battalion relieved the 11th K.O.R.L. in the LEFT SUBSECTOR, VILLERS PLOUICH and BEAUCAMP SECTORS. Battalion headquarters established at the junction of LINCOLN AVENUE and the INTERMEDIATE LINE. FRONT. RIGHT. "D" Coy. CENTRE. "B" Coy. LEFT. "C" Coy. SUPPORT. "A" Coy.	
	11.8.17		Patrols of 1 Officer and 8 O.R. from each Company patrolled No Man's Land throughout the hours of darkness. Enemy gun line from R.7.6.5.5, 1 machine / front-line and BEAUCAMP - RIBECOURT road. Work from PLOSH TRENCH reaching BOAR COPSE and BEAUCAMP - RIBECOURT road. Unoccupied. Very few or no signs of the enemy. Entrenched the ... of RIBECOURT in front of BEAUCAMP SUPPORT and OXFORD LANE (un detected held on the latter	

A3834 Wt. W4973 M687 730,000 8/16 D. D. & L. Ltd. Forms/C.2118/13.

Army Form C. 2118.

WAR DIARY

or

INTELLIGENCE SUMMARY.

(Erase heading not required.)

13th BATTALION
EAST SURREY REGIMENT.

Instructions regarding War Diaries and Intelligence
Summaries are contained in F. S. Regs., Part II.
and the Staff Manual respectively. Title pages
will be prepared in manuscript.

120th BRIGADE
40th DIVISION.

Place	Date	Hour	Summary of Events and Information	Remarks and references to Appendices
	12.8.17		Hostile artillery fired 20 rounds 77mm into BEAUCAMP and 12 rounds 77mm into BOAR COPSE from direction of RIBECOURT at 9am. Offr. patrols of 1 Officer and 6 OR left each Company front on R7a or 57, Q6d.20 and Q6c.13. No enemy patrols encountered. Enemy now very quiet. Lt.Col. Martin to Hospital. Hunt to Ardeen to command Battalion	[signature]
	13.8.17		Offr. patrols (1 Officer and 7 OR) left each Company front. No mans land patrolled throughout the term of darkness. No hostile patrols were encountered. Intermittent shelling of RIBECOURT throughout the day. Enemy shelled BEAUCAMP and VILLAGE SPROES during the afternoon with 77mm. One direct hit on the trench at 5 pm. his Light T.M. fired on BOAR COPSE. E.A active, and fired Machine gun into our trenches	[signature]
	14.8.17		Relief: C.S.S Cops left for England. Battalion relieved by the 11th No.R. about 4 pm 'A'Coy & VILLERS PLOUCH 'C'B'COY INTERMEDIATE LINE 'D' Coy and HQ L 15 RAVINE	[signature]

13ᵗʰ BATTALION
EAST SURREY REGIMENT 120ᵗʰ BRIGADE
40ᵗʰ DIVISION.

WAR DIARY
or
INTELLIGENCE SUMMARY.

(Erase heading not required.)

Army Form C. 2118.

Instructions regarding War Diaries and Intelligence
Summaries are contained in F. S. Regs., Part II.
and the Staff Manual respectively. Title pages
will be prepared in manuscript.

Place	Date	Hour	Summary of Events and Information	Remarks and references to Appendices
	15.5.17		Parade under Company arrangements 2/Lieut. R.H.F. Peacock joined the Battalion	
	16.5.17		Parades according to Battalion programme.	
	17.5.17		Platoon and Company inspections according to programme.	
	18.5.17		Lieut Col H.L. Warden. Northumberland Fusiliers, joined the Battalion. Parades under Company arrangements	
	19.5.17		2/Lieuts R.W.Vaile and C.E. Simpson joined the Battalion. Battalion warned for relief	

A5834 Wt. W4973 M687 730,000 8/16 D. D. & L. Ltd. Forms/C.2118/13.

Army Form C. 2118.

WAR DIARY

or

INTELLIGENCE SUMMARY.

(Erase heading not required.)

Instructions regarding War Diaries and Intelligence Summaries are contained in F. S. Regs., Part II. and the Staff Manual respectively. Title pages will be prepared in manuscript.

13th BATTALION
EAST SURREY REGIMENT.
120th BRIGADE
40th DIVISION

Place	Date	Hour	Summary of Events and Information	Remarks and references to Appendices
	26.8.17		The Battalion relieved the 11th K.O.R.L. in the left Sub-sector, VILLERS PLOUICH, and BEAUCAMP SECTORS during the afternoon. Front Right 'A' Coy Centre 'B' Coy Left 'C' Coy Support Company 'D' Coy. Battalion H.Q. established at Q.18.6.8.5. Part of 1 Officer and 12 O.R. left our lines at 8.P.7 a 30.40 at 9.15 p.m. BOHR COPSE and intet front reached. No hostile patrol. Saw encountered. Enemy quiet.	[initials]
	21.8.17		Observation kept throughout the day, from Q.6.c 35.70 Camouflaged pot-inspected at Q.6.d.19. Four enemy seen at intervals without hostile tanks. Two standing patrols of 1 NCO and 6 O.R. advanced at R.1.c.50.10, and Q.6.c.45.75. Patrol of 1 Officer and 15 O.R. left on tour at Q.6.d.21. at 9 p.m. BOHR COPSE and RAVINE. O.i.a wounded. No sign of enemy.	[initials]
	22.8.17		Standing patrol of 1 NCO. and 6 O.R. went out at points Q.6.c.47. and Q.6.d.24. throughout the night. Enemy Machine gun fire from Q.6.b.15. Patrol of 1 Officer and 15 O.R. left on line at junction of first line and	

A.5834 Wt. W.4973 M.687 750,000 8/16 D. D. & L. Ltd. Forms/C.2118/13.

WAR DIARY

or

INTELLIGENCE SUMMARY.

(Erase heading not required.)

13th BATTALION
EAST SURREY REGIMENT.
120th BRIGADE
40th DIVISION

Instructions regarding War Diaries and Intelligence
Summaries are contained in F. S. Regs. Part II.
and the Staff Manual respectively. Title pages
will be prepared in manuscript.

Place	Date	Hour	Summary of Events and Information	Remarks and references to Appendices
	22.8.17	(P.M.)	R.I.S. Court road. Patrol approached enemy trap at R.1.c.15.05. and was fired on. Bomb corps and Rarini. Q.6.a.51. searched, and shewing in Q.6.a. Unoccupied. Patrol turned E. and reached about R.6.b.3.0. when a shower of bombs fell among them. Casualties. Pte. C.B. Rice and J.O.R. wounded. 2463 Sgt. Ratcliff J. Mann. 20042 Pte. Foucher F.G.	
	23.8.17		Patrol 1 Officer and 25 O.R. took Keere Gun. left our line at 9.15 p.m. Keere Q.6.c.4.3. Patol turned forward to Rarini c.Q.6.a.51. which was found Unoccupied. Searching patol of 16 O.R. dropped to S. end of Rarini and remainder searched Rarini front. No enemy met. Lieut. Col. W.C. Martin, Evacuated to England (Sick)	
	24.8.17		Enemy artillery shelled front line about O.R. a 9.1. a.6.55.a.m. 3 wounded. 77 mm. enemy active in PLUSH TRENCH about R.1.c.5.8 active 7.30 a.m. then seen passing N of R.I.S. Court. Patrol 1 NCO and 6 O.R. left from line at Q.6.c.5.2. Bomb corps not occupied. and Battalion front. Unoccupied. No enemy encountered.	

A5834 Wt. W4973 M687 730,000 8/16 D. D. & L. Ltd. Forms/C.2113/13.

WAR DIARY

or

INTELLIGENCE SUMMARY.

(Erase heading not required.)

13ᵗʰ BATTALION
EAST SURREY REGIMENT
120ᵗʰ BRIGADE
40ᵗʰ DIVISION

Instructions regarding War Diaries and Intelligence
Summaries are contained in F. S. Regs., Part II.
and the Staff Manual respectively. Title pages
will be prepared in manuscript.

Place	Date	Hour	Summary of Events and Information	Remarks and references to Appendices
	25.8.17		Situation kept throughout the day. Aim. S'mt of Boar Copse. Standing patrols l/15th in 9.6.d 30.35 and Q.6.c.85 throughout the night. Patrol 5.10 pm. 15 O.R. officer being at 10.10 pm. R.7. a.5.7. in conjunction with patrol 6. 14 K.A. F.S.H. Ground in front cleared but no enemy found.	[signature]
	26.8.17		Battalion relieved at 2.30 pm by 14th M.G.R. and withdrew to Brigade Reserve. Battalion Headquarters in Gouzeaucourt Wood	[signature]
	27.8.17		Parades under Company arrangement. 2/Lieut A.W. Gill rejoined the Battalion. Lieut C.J. Hepburn joined the Battalion.	[signature]
	28.8.17		Company and Platoon inspections according to Battalion programme	[signature]
	29.8.17		Training & Company parades according to Battalion programme. No.26785 A/Cpl Cartwright A.E. awarded the MILITARY MEDAL. On the night 22/23rd Aug. he found part of a Patrol isolated. Suffered heavy casualties. He was greatly instrumental in bringing back six wounded to our lines, and throughout displayed great courage and enterprise.	[signature]

A5834. Wt. W4973 M687 750,000 8/16 D. D. & L. Ltd. Forms/C.2118/13.

Army Form C. 2118.

WAR DIARY

or

~~INTELLIGENCE~~ SUMMARY.

(Erase heading not required.)

13ᵗʰ Battalion
Eᴀsт Surrey Regiment
120ᵗʰ Brigade
40ᵗʰ Division

Instructions regarding War Diaries and Intelligence Summaries are contained in F. S. Regs., Part II. and the Staff Manual respectively. Title pages will be prepared in manuscript.

Place	Date	Hour	Summary of Events and Information	Remarks and references to Appendices
	30.5.17.		Parades under Company arrangements according to Battalion programme.	
	31.5.17		Platoon and Company training according to Battalion programme. Lecture by Commanding Officer to Officers, Warrant Officers, and N.C.O.s.	

H. Warden
Lt. Col.

Commanding 13ᵗʰ Battalion
East Surrey Regiment

A5834 Wt. W4973 M687 750,000 8/16 D. D. & L. Ltd. Forms/C.2118/13.

Vol 16

E.W.

16.D
12 sheets

13ᵗʰ Battn. East Surrey Regt.

WAR DIARY

For Month Ending

30ᵗʰ September 1917

WAR DIARY

or

INTELLIGENCE SUMMARY.

(Erase heading not required.)

• /13th BATTALION
EAST SURREY REGIMENT.
120th BRIGADE   VOL XVI
40th DIVISION

Instructions regarding War Diaries and Intelligence
Summaries are contained in F. S. Regs., Part II.
and the Staff Manual respectively. Title pages
will be prepared in manuscript.

Place	Date	Hour	Summary of Events and Information	Remarks and references to Appendices
BEAUCAMP	1.9.17		The Battn relieved the 11th K.O.R.L. in the LEFT SUBSECTOR VILLERS PLOUICH and BEAUCAMP Sector in the afternoon. Dispositions:- Right: Centre: Left: Support:- Coy. D Coy. A Coy B Coy Batt. Headquarters established at Q.18.c.55. The Commanding Officer presented the ribbon of the MILITARY MEDAL to No 25305 Pte Castang H. A.E.	[signature]
	2.9.17.		Standing patrols of 1 Officer and 20 O.R., 1 N.C.O. and 6 O.R. and 1 Officer and 20 O.R. left the right Centre and Left Company fronts respectively, and remained during the hours of darkness at points R.1.c.50, Q.6.d.37 and Q.6.a.71. Party of 6 enemy seen near PLUSH TRENCH about R.1.c.55 and some obey fire they retired towards a 5 minutes Enemy shelled at during day in and behind PLUSH TRENCH	[signature]
	3.9.17.		Artillery very quiet. Standing patrols left each Company front. Got up positions at R.1.c.52, Q.6.d.37, Q.6.c.35.90, Q.6.c.05.15. Very very clear, went to Hythair Common. Found spread heard from Crater R.36.c.05.15. No enemy patrols encountered.	[signature]

A5834   Wt. W4973 M687 750,000 8/16 D. D. & L. Ltd. Forms/C.2118/13.

13ᵗʰ BATTALION
EAST SURREY REGIMENT.
120ᵗʰ BRIGADE
40ᵗʰ DIVISION.

WAR DIARY
or
INTELLIGENCE SUMMARY.

(Erase heading not required.)

Instructions regarding War Diaries and Intelligence
Summaries are contained in F. S. Regs., Part II.
and the Staff Manual respectively. Title pages
will be prepared in manuscript.

VOL XVI

Place	Date	Hour	Summary of Events and Information	Remarks and references to Appendices
BEAUCAMP	4.9.17.		Standing Patrols from each front Company took up positions during the hours of darkness. MG fire fairly active. No enemy seen. 2 incendiary flares "a" in Bn. Front. RAWNE "a Q.6.a. 1020 unoccupied. Found M.m.g. gun. Went from Crater K.36.c.05.15. at 16.30. an. party of inhabitants saw observed working in trench about L.31. & 4.4. L.G. and 3 magazines. Enemy was observed carrying in Cover the Party returned on 4.9. and casualties about 12.	
	5.9.17.		Lt. F.W. Scott awarded the Military Cross. By the night of 22/23ʳᵈ August 1917. Lieut. Scott displayed complete disregard for danger and showed initiative and devotion. On hearing that an Officers Patrol of the Regiment had suffered casualties and that men were missing. Although wounded he went out In sweeping trenches. Unaware of same known, and carried heard parties. To find the missing men. Moral Standing Patrols posted. Facing my front during the 24 hours.	
	6.9.17.		Standing Patrols of 1 Officer and 20 oR, 1NCO and 6 o.R. and 1 Officer, and 15oR and 2 G. Left own line and took up positions about R1.c.5.7, Q1.d.35.60, Q.6.a.5.1. The night was exceptionally quiet. Enemy trench mortar about K.35.c bombarded for about 30 minutes from 9.45 p.m. to Q.6.d.9.6.95. Sniper Claim Rct. about Q.6.d.9.6.95.	

A5834 Wt.W4973 M687 730,000 8/16 D. D. & L. Ltd. Forms/C.2118/13.

13th BATTALION
EAST SURREY REGIMENT
1/20th BRIGADE
40th DIVISION

WAR DIARY
or
INTELLIGENCE SUMMARY.   VOL XVI

Instructions regarding War Diaries and Intelligence
Summaries are contained in F. S. Regs., Part II.
and the Staff Manual respectively. Title pages
will be prepared in manuscript.

(Erase heading not required.)

Place	Date	Hour	Summary of Events and Information	Remarks and references to Appendices
BEAUCAMP.	7.9.17		In the afternoon the Battn returned to support, and relieved the 14th H.L.I., being relieved by 13th K.O.L.I. Battn H.Q. and C Coy in FIFTEEN RAVINE D " R. 13 a. 8 4. (VILLERS PLOUGH) A - INTERMEDIATE LINE @ 15.c B - CHARING CROSS.	/mil/
FIFTEEN RAVINE.	8.9.17		Parades made. Company arrangements. Working parties in right and left Battalions.	/mil/
	9.9.17		Parades according to Battalion programme. 2nd Lieut. R.H. Rowland rejoined the Battalion from Hospital	/mil/
	10.9.17.		Work in Left Battalion according to programme.	/mil/

A 5834 Wt. W4973 M687 750,000 8/16 D. D. & L. Ltd. Forms/C.2118/13.

WAR DIARY
or
INTELLIGENCE SUMMARY.

(Erase heading not required.)

13th BATTALION
EAST SURREY REGIMENT
Intelligence 120th BRIGADE
Title pages 40th DIVISION.

Instructions regarding War Diaries and Intelligence Summaries are contained in F. S. Regs., Part II. and the Staff Manual respectively. Title pages will be prepared in manuscript.

VOL XVI

Place	Date	Hour	Summary of Events and Information	Remarks and references to Appendices
FIFTEEN RAVINE	11.9.17 (Ctd)		Usual programme of work according to scheme.	
	12.9.17		Training. In relief of the Left Battalion.	
BEAUCAMP	13.9.17		In the afternoon the Battalion relieved the 11th R. Lanc. Reg't in the left Subsector. VILLERS PLOUICH and BEAUCAMP Sectors. A Company Right Front. B Company Centre. D Company Left. C Company Support.	
	14.9.17		Patrol of 1 Officer and 16 OR left on line at R.7 a.40.35 at 8.30 pm. Advanced to bombing pit at R.1.g.35.70. On approaching enemy's line. Verbal sent on from the right Battn front. Man detached. No enemy patrols encountered. Patrol returned at 1.45 am. Party observed working our forget new road at R.1.d.1.4. Fired at but not claimed. Enemy aircraft took active.	

A5834 Wt. W4973 M687 750,000 8/16. D. D. & L. Ltd. Forms/C.2118/13.

13th BATTALION
EAST SURREY REGIMENT 120th BRIGADE
40th DIVISION

WAR DIARY
or
INTELLIGENCE SUMMARY. VOL XVI

(Erase heading not required.)

Instructions regarding War Diaries and Intelligence Summaries are contained in F. S. Regs., Part II. and the Staff Manual respectively. Title pages will be prepared in manuscript.

Place	Date	Hour	Summary of Events and Information	Remarks and references to Appendices
BEAUCAMP.	15.9.17		Hostile artillery shelled in front of BANVILLE and GRANTHAM POSTS during day with 77mm. BONE COPSE shelled during day with 77mm from direction of FIRECOURT. 745pm. Enemy heavy Trench Mortar turn about K.24.d. Patrol J. Officer and 1 OR left on line from Q.6.c.4.2. BONE COPSE, RAVINE and SPINNEY searched and found unoccupied. Enemy patrol seen west of the Ravine. No Enemy Encountered.	◯◯◯◯*
	16.9.17		Standing patrol on R.BECOURT Rd. at Q.6.d.25.40. during the morning. Walking wounded Report: Patrol 1/ Officer and 18 OR left line at Q.6.a.70.16 at 5 p.m. and searched RAVINE + SPINNEY. No Signs of Enemy. H.V. Gun fired down the morning the direction of BOURLON WOOD. Blacks and khaki patrols observed from PLUSH TRENCH at N1.d.50.05. Lt. R.D. MacGregor RNMI relieved Capt. G.R. Spence RAMC — to England.	◯◯◯◯*
	17.9.17		Mutual hostility front. Patrol 1/1 Officer and 18 OR regimental 8th front to enemy. Patrol encountered enemy artillery less active. 8th claimed at L.31.8.9.0. 1.15 p.m. his frame behind MISP.O.ING.	◯◯◯◯*
	18.9.17		Enemy artillery normal. Heliograph again observed signalling at L.21.8.29 at 1.35 pm. Parties of enemy working about L.28.a.28. Patrol 1/1 Officer and 16 OR left on line from Q.12.b.50.75. Left post formed about Q.6.d.53.90. Pierced 2 enemy posts at Q.6.d.85.95. Had saw no signs of enemy. Returned at 3.45 am. Listening post at Q.6.d.25.40.	◯◯◯◯*

A5834 Wt.W4973 M687 750,000 8/16 D. D. & L. Ltd. Forms/C.2118/13.

Army Form C. 2118.

WAR DIARY
or
INTELLIGENCE SUMMARY.

(Erase heading not required.)

13th EAST SURREY REGIMENT. 120th BRIGADE. VOL. XVI
40th DIVISION

Instructions regarding War Diaries and Intelligence Summaries are contained in F. S. Regs., Part II. and the Staff Manual respectively. Title pages will be prepared in manuscript.

Place	Date	Hour	Summary of Events and Information	Remarks and references to Appendices
BEAUCAMP	19.9.17		In the afternoon, the Battalion was relieved by the 11th R. Lanc Regiment and northern to Brigade Reserve. Disposition - Headquarters, B and C Coy GOUZEAUCOURT WOOD. D Coy DESSART WOOD. A Coy CHARING CROSS	
			'A' Company was sent to orders of the O.C. 14th A.S.H. until relieved by a company of that Battalion on the 20th. 2nd Lieut G.E. Acason rejoined the Battalion from ÉTAPLES	
	20.9.17		Parades under Company arrangements. Company and Platoon inspections.	
	21.9.17		Musketry and Platoon training under Battalion arrangements.	
	22.9.17		Platoon and Company training according to Battalion programme. Lecture by Commanding officer to all officers	

A5834 Wt.W4973/M1687 750,000 8/16 D.D. & L. Ltd. Forms/C.2118/13.

13th BATTALION
EAST SURREY REGIMENT.
II / 120th BRIGADE
40th DIVISION

WAR DIARY

or

INTELLIGENCE SUMMARY.   VOL. XVI

(*Erase heading not required.*)

Army Form C. 2118.

Instructions regarding War Diaries and Intelligence
Summaries are contained in F. S. Regs., Part II.
and the Staff Manual respectively. Title pages
will be prepared in manuscript.

Place	Date	Hour	Summary of Events and Information	Remarks and references to Appendices
	23.9.17		Ceremonial drill preparatory to Corps Commanders presentation of rewards. Company Commander	
	24.9.17		Battalion band made the Commanding Officer at DESSART WOOD. Lieut. A.G.J. Altman joined the Battalion	
	25.9.17		In the morning the Battalion paraded for the presentation by the Corps Commander of rewards of the MILITARY CROSS to Lieut V.H.Scott and 2/Lieut. J.W.Wilson. At 5 pm the Battalion relieved the 11th R. Sussex Regt in the Left Subsector, BEAUCAMP and VILLERS PLOUICH Sect.	
			D Coy Right Front	
			B Coy Centre Front	
			C Coy Left Front	
			A Coy Support	

A 5834   Wt. W4973/M687 750,000 8/16   D. D. & L. Ltd.   Forms/C.2118/13.

Army Form C. 2118.

13ᵗʰ BATTALION
EAST SURREY REGIMENT
120ᵗʰ BRIGADE
40ᵗʰ DIVISION

WAR DIARY
or
INTELLIGENCE SUMMARY.   VOL. XVI

(Erase heading not required.)

Instructions regarding War Diaries and Intelligence
Summaries are contained in F. S. Regs., Part II.
and the Staff Manual respectively. Title pages
will be prepared in manuscript.

Place	Date	Hour	Summary of Events and Information	Remarks and references to Appendices
BEAUCAMP	25.9.17		Patrol of 1 Officer and 17 OR before lines from Q.12.d.35.90 at 11 p.m. Patrol moved N. as far as R.1.a.2.2. Battalion front patrolled as far as Q.6. Central. On reaching point about Q.6.a.9.1 a shower of bombs fell on N. lip E. edge of RAVINE Q.6.a.80.15. 15 mins later enemy bombed his own front at Q.6.b.26.30. RAVINE searched and found unoccupied. Patrol returned at 2.45 a.m. Slight artillery activity on front and support lines 9 Right Company at 8 p.m.	[initials]
	26.9.17		Hostile artillery more active. Lds. Mins. on BORR COPSE at 1 p.m. COALVILLE and BROOKSBY Post shelled during the evening with 77mm. From direction of COUILLET WOOD between 5 p.m. and 5.30 p.m. junction of BEAUCAMP SWITCH and YORK AVENUE shelled with 4.2 and 77mm. Patrol 1/1 Officer and 17 OR left our line from Q.6.c.o.2 at midnight. BORR COPSE searched. Patrol moved E. as far as Q.6.a.56.18 where enemy patrol of 6 OR was left. 5 enemy opened fire. Turn unsuccessful at Q.6.a.9.2 more N.E. An attempt was made to cut them off in the SPINNEY. Enemy turned E. and disappeared. Patrol fired on from about Q.6.6.2.A. Returned at 4.45 a.m. Offensive patrols 1/1 NCO 6 OR harassed all points, R.7.a.4.9, R.1.c.o.o, and Q.6.d.25.40.0 ARGYLL ROAD during the hours 9 darkness. Nothing unusual to report.	[initials]

13th BATTALION
EAST SURREY REGIMENT
124th BRIGADE
41st DIVISION

VOL XVI

WAR DIARY
or
INTELLIGENCE SUMMARY.

(Erase heading not required.)

Instructions regarding War Diaries and Intelligence
Summaries are contained in F. S. Regs., Part II.
and the Staff Manual respectively. Title pages
will be prepared in manuscript.

Place	Date	Hour	Summary of Events and Information	Remarks and references to Appendices
BEAUCAMP	27.9.17		Patrol of 1 Officer and 19 OR left our line at Q.6.d.2.0. at 11 p.m. On reaching point about Q.6.d.30.90. patrol was fired on by M.G. and 2½ [?] fire directed of Q.6.B.40.35. Attacked party of 6 OR was sent N. from this point. The scene Lieut. M.G. [?] in d. at and d.6. Central. The Lieut. S.E. and Patrolled Battalion front. No enemy patrols encountered. Patrol returned at 4.15 a.m. Standing patrol of 1 N.C.O. & 6 OR stayed at Q.6.d.3.4. during daylight. No Enemy seen or heard. At 6.30 p.m. one enemy man walking in pairs in front of PLUSH TRENCH about Q.6.6.05.65. He fell when fired upon. Not observed. Junction 1 BEAUCAMP SWITCH and YORK AVENUE shelled 11.10 p.m. — 11.40 p.m. about 4.2	
	28.9.17		Headquarters of 1 N.C.O. & 5 O.R. manned at Q.6.d.2.6.5.35 during the night. No enemy seen or heard. Hostile artillery activity about BOAR COPSE & vicinity at intervals between 2.30 p.m. & 11 p.m. Our trenches in the [...] OXFORD POST & BROOKSBY POST, OXFORD BANK & [...] of RIDGECOURT. By HQ 17 men returned and from direction of RIDGECOURT. At [...] enemy observed about R.14.c.3.9. thought [...] at 5.0. Raiding party [...] to [...] the [...] ... for [...] north of PLUSH TRENCH at R.1.d.1.6. at 10.15 a.m. Quite some smoke [...] of [...] ... Lewis gun is directed in PLUSH TRENCH at Q.6.a.9.8.20. [...] patrol [...] while operations [...] followed by [...]	

A5834 Wt.W4973/M687 750,000 8/16 D. D. & L. Ltd. Forms/C.2118/13.

Instructions regarding War Diaries and Intelligence
Summaries are contained in F. S. Regs., Part II.
and the Staff Manual respectively. Title pages
will be prepared in manuscript.

Army Form C. 2118.

WAR DIARY
or
INTELLIGENCE SUMMARY.

(Erase heading not required.)

13th BATTALION
EAST SURREY REGIMENT
120th BRIGADE
40th DIVISION

VOL. XVI

Place	Date	Hour	Summary of Events and Information	Remarks and references to Appendices
BEAUCAMP	29.9.17		Standing patrol of 1 N.C.O. & 4 O.R. posts at Q.6.a.x 5.35. during the night.	
			Working parties as usual.	
			Our Lewis Guns active from positions... during the night. Enemy guns harassed ... intervals during the night on RANSART ... X.4.15 p.m. our guns opened rapid fire at ... B.32.c.7.3. ... Lieut. W. A. MORRIS. Battalion rejoining TRUSH TRENCH at R.1.d.2.4. St. VAAST. — SUR. SOMME	⟨signature⟩
	30.9.17		Standing patrol & remainder ... Our Lewis Guns active ... Enemy guns harassed ... during the night ... Harris Battery ... of LEICESTER Av. 14 ... OXFORD & QUEEN'S POSTS & BOAR COPSE. ... direction of RIBECOURT. 9.15 a.m. ... 10.20 a.m. ... 4.15 p.m. ... TRUSH TRENCH at R.1.d.2.5. ... at 6.15 p.m. ... about R.1.P.6. ... FUSILIERS	⟨signature⟩

A 834 Wt. W4973/M687 750,000 8/16 D. D. & L. Ltd. Forms/C.2118/13.

Army Form C. 2118.

10 Battalion
East Surrey Regiment
1/10 Brigade
40 Division

WAR DIARY

or

INTELLIGENCE SUMMARY.

(Erase heading not required.)

VOL. XVI

Instructions regarding War Diaries and Intelligence
Summaries are contained in F. S. Regs. Part II
and the Staff Manual respectively. Title pages
will be prepared in manuscript.

Place	Date	Hour	Summary of Events and Information	Remarks and references to Appendices
BEAUCAMP	30.9.19	-	5 p.m. two hostile aeroplanes crossed over our lines. But fire was opened on them. Two hostile flying in direction of CAMBRAI. Casualties 5 Wounded.	

M.H. _____
Comdg. 13th Battalion
East Surrey Regiment. 1/10/17.

A 5834 Wt. W.4973/M687 750,000 8/16 D. D. & L. Ltd. Forms/C.2118/13.

YM 17

17. D.
8 sheets

WAR DIARY

OF THE

13TH BN. EAST SURREY REGT.

VOLUME II

FOR THE MONTH OF OCTOBER 1917

Army Form C. 2118.

13th Battalion.
East Surrey Regiment WAR DIARY
or
120th Brigade INTELLIGENCE SUMMARY
40th Division

Instructions regarding War Diaries and Intelligence Summaries are contained in F. S. Regs., Part II. and the Staff Manual respectively. Title pages will be prepared in manuscript.

(Erase heading not required.)

Place	Date	Hour	Summary of Events and Information	Remarks and references to Appendices
BEAUCAMP	1/10/17		In the afternoon the Battalion withdrew to support and relieved 15th H.L.I. being relieved by the 11th K.O.R.L. Batt. HQ. and B Coy in FIFTEEN RAVINE C Coy - R.13.a.P.H. (VILLERS PLOUICH) D " - INTERMEDIATE LINE (Q.18.c.a.d) A " = CHARING CROSS.	
FIFTEEN RAVINE	2/10/17	-	Parades were Company arranged. Working parties to Right & Left Battalion.	
	3/10/17	-	Company Parades. Working parties for front line Battalion.	
	4/10/17	-	Working Parties according to Programme. In the afternoon Representatives of the 12th Rifle Brigade came to reconnoitre, prior to relieving us on 5th Inst.	

A5834 Wt.W4973/M687 750,000 8/16 D.D.&L Ltd. Forms/C.2118/13.

Army Form C. 2118.

WAR DIARY
or
INTELLIGENCE SUMMARY.

(Erase heading not required.)

Instructions regarding War Diaries and Intelligence
Summaries are contained in F. S. Regs. Part II.
and the Staff Manual respectively. Title pages
will be prepared in manuscript.

13ᵗʰ Battalion
East Surrey Regiment
1/20 Inf Brigade
HQ 5 Division

Place	Date	Hour	Summary of Events and Information	Remarks and references to Appendices
FITTEN RAVINE	5/10/17	.	In the morning the Batt. was relieved by the 11ᵗʰ Rifle Brigade, 60ᵗʰ Division & in turn proceeded to camp at HEUDECOURT (SorEL AREA), when the Batt. took over from 6ᵗʰ Oxon & Bucks Light Infantry, 20ᵗʰ Division.	D/4
HEUDECOURT (Camp)	6/10/17	.	Battalion marched by Coy to PERONNE & was billeted in civil homes.	D/5
PERONNE	7/10/17	.	Church Parade in the morning. Remainder of the day was a Company arrangement. Under G.R.O. No. 254, dated 1/9/17, the C.O. authorized the following Officers to wear badges of rank of temporary Lieutenant:— 2/Lt J.E.M. CROWTHER. Lt R.H.T. PEACOCK. ,, J.W. WILSON. ,, A.C. THOMPSON. ,, W.R.B. HUGHES. ,, W.A. MORRIS. ,, A.W. GIBB. ,, G.E. DEACON. ,, W.A. ANDREW. ,, L.W. PINNICK. ,, R.N.H. KING. ,, C.M. JAMES.	D/6

A5834 Wt. W4973/M687 750,000 8/16 D. D. & L. Ltd. Forms/C.2118/13.

13th Battalion
East Surrey Regiment
121 Inf. Brigade
40th Division

Instructions regarding War Diaries and Intelligence
Summaries are contained in F. S. Regs., Part II
and the Staff Manual respectively. Title pages
will be prepared in manuscript.

Place	Date	Hour	Summary of Events and Information	Remarks and references to Appendices
PERONNE	7/10/17	—	The following appointments were made in the Battalion:— Capt. J.R. Hucker relinquishes the appt. of Instr. Regtl. Adjutant in consequence of his being in command of "B" Coy. of ... Lieut. G.E. Deacon to be Orderly Room Adjutant Lieut. G. Beaumont — Brigade Gas Officer " F.H. Whitcroft " Orderly Officer " A.W. Pinnick " Signalling Officer (temporarily)	[signature] 8/16
	8/10/17		In the morning about three hundred recruits were ... under Company arrangements. Reveille routine ... in the afternoon all of the Brigade in the Hippodrome, PERONNE, for an inspection and march past by the Corps Commander.	[signature] 8/16
	9/10/17		In the afternoon the Batt. entrained at PERONNE Station & were by rail to DOULLENS ... [via] DOISLEUX au MONT. Batt. was marched to BIENVILLE [BRANCHVILLE] arriving there in the early hours of the morning. By reason of this move the Battalion is transferred from the 5th Corps to VII Corps.	[signature] 8/16

A5834 Wt. W4973/M687 750,000 8/16 D. D. & L. Ltd. Forms/C.2118/13.

13th Battalion
East Surrey Regt.

WAR DIARY
or
INTELLIGENCE SUMMARY.

(Erase heading not required.)

Instructions regarding War Diaries and Intelligence
Summaries are contained in F. S. Regs., Part II.
and the Staff Manual respectively. Title pages
will be prepared in manuscript.

Intelligence/120th Inf. Bde.
40th Division

Place	Date	Hour	Summary of Events and Information	Remarks and references to Appendices
BLARGIES	10/10/17	—	Parade was Company arrangements. Instructed to clearing up after the long period the Battalion has had in the trenches.	
	11/10/17		Parades according to Battalion & Brigade Programme.	
	12/10/17		Parades in accordance with the scheme of training laid down in Brigade & Battalion Programme.	
	13/10/17		Battalion paraded for Church parade at 11.30 a.m. Battalion Concert in the evening.	
	14/10/17		Parades according to Battalion Programme.	
	15/10/17		Lieut. W. G. Rice attended the Quartermaster. Parade according to Programme. Lecture to Officers and N.C.O.s by the Commanding Officer at 5 p.m.	

A3834 Wt. W4973/M687 750,000 8/16 D. D. & L. Ltd. Forms/C.2118/13.

13ᵗʰ BATTALION
EAST SURREY REGIMENT

WAR DIARY

or

INTELLIGENCE SUMMARY.

(Erase heading not required.)

Instructions regarding War Diaries and Intelligence
Summaries are contained in F. S. Regs., Part II.
and the Staff Manual respectively. Title pages
will be prepared in manuscript.

124 BRIGADE
41ˢᵗ DIVISION

Place	Date	Hour	Summary of Events and Information	Remarks and references to Appendices
BERNEVILLE	16.10.17		Parade as per Ly. Notes. Action by the Commanding Officer, H.O's and NCO's at 5.30.p.m.	
	17.10.17		Battalion paraded at 8 a.m. and marched to CROISX (R.23.c.67.) Training in Companies in the attack	
	18.10.17		Battalion marched to WAILLY. Tactical exercises in trench attack from the Old British Front line.	
	19.10.17		Company training and MUSKETRY according to Syllabus. 41st Division transferred from VII Corps to III Corps from 12 noon October 18ᵗʰ.	
	20.10.17		Battalion Relieved in trench attack at training area. R.15. a.m. & aft't	
	21.10.17		Battalion Church Parade at M.O. a.m. Battalion Sports at 1.30 p.m.	

A5834   Wt. W4973/M687   750,000   8/16   D. D. & L. Ltd.   Forms/C.2118/13.

Army Form C. 2118.

13TH BATTALION
EAST SURREY REGIMENT
120th BRIGADE 40th Division

WAR DIARY

or

INTELLIGENCE SUMMARY.

(Erase heading not required.)

Instructions regarding War Diaries and Intelligence Summaries are contained in F. S. Regs., Part II. and the Staff Manual respectively. Title pages will be prepared in manuscript.

Place	Date	Hour	Summary of Events and Information	Remarks and references to Appendices
BERNEVILLE	22.10.17		Battalion training in trench attack at R.23.24.29.30	
	23.10.17		A & B. Companies carried in lorries training at SOUASTRE. C & D Companies training trenches at BERNEVILLE.	
	24.10.17		Parades according to Battalion programme.	
	25.10.17		Practice in trench attack in conjunction with 14th R.H.L.I. in R.29	Ref. M.M. 51.C.S.E. 1/20,000 M.M.
	26.10.17		Company training in "musketry" according to programme.	
	27.10.17		Parades according to Schedule.	

Army Form C. 2118.

WAR DIARY

or

INTELLIGENCE SUMMARY.

(Erase heading not required.)

13ᵗʰ BATTALION
EAST SURREY REGIMENT
120ᵗʰ Brigade
40ᵗʰ Division.

Instructions regarding War Diaries and Intelligence
Summaries are contained in F. S. Regs., Part II.
and the Staff Manual respectively. Title pages
will be prepared in manuscript.

Place	Date	Hour	Summary of Events and Information	Remarks and references to Appendices
BERNEVILLE	28.10.17		Battalion Church Parade at 9 a.m. Final Match for Divisional Cup between 14ᵗʰ A.P.L.I. and 21ˢᵗ Middlesex Regiments at GOUY-EN-ARTOIS at 11.30 a.m.	
	29.10.17		Battalion marched to billets in GRENAS via BEAUMETZ-LÉS-LOGES, MONDICOURT and POMMERA. Battn and Company H.Q.s in the Chateau GRENTS.	
	30.10.17		Parade and Company Marcyments.	
	31.10.17		Parades and Company Marcyments.	

A5834 Wt. W4973/M687 750,000 8/16 D. D. & L. Ltd. Forms/C.2118/13.

Major
Commanding 13ᵗʰ Battalion East Surrey Regiment.

SUBJECT.

No.	Contents.	Date.

War Diary

of

13ᵗʰ E. Surrey

~~Battalion~~

for Nov. 1917

(63,965). Wt.15,820—176. 2000. 9/21. Gp.164. A.&E.W.

Vol 18

Wo/20

WAR DIARY

OF THE

13ᵀᴴ Bⁿ EAST SURREY REGT.

VOLUME XVIII.

FOR THE MONTH OF NOVEMBER 1917

18 D.
16 sheets

13th Battalion.
East Surrey Regiment / 120th Inf. Bde.
40th Division

WAR DIARY   VOLUME XVIII

— or —

INTELLIGENCE SUMMARY.

(Erase heading not required.)

Instructions regarding War Diaries and Intelligence
Summaries are contained in F. S. Regs., Part II.
and the Staff Manual respectively. Title pages
will be prepared in manuscript.

Place	Date	Hour	Summary of Events and Information	Remarks and references to Appendices
GREVILLERS	1/11/17		Company Parades. Practicing an attack on a strong point. HURTEBISE FARM Area. Lieut R.H.H.KING proceeds on 14 days leave to England.	
	2/11/17		Battalion attack, practising to working on A–B area HURTEBISE Farm. Lieut Col. H.L. WARDEN resumed command of the Battalion after commanding the 120 the Inf. Bde. (on from 25.10.17) in the absence of Brig-General the C.H.S.D. WILLOUGHBY on leave. Capt. W.C.T. KEDDIE M.C. 14th Royal Welsh Fusiliers attached to the Bn. attached to the Bn. promoted Acting Major on from 27.10.17. & in command of 2 B. in town 11 October 1917.	
	3/11/17		Parades at the disposal of Company Commanders in the vicinity of Billets. Special training with Lewis Guns & Officers. Lieut. L.W PINNICK proceeds on 14 days leave to England & and 2nd Lieut. F.N. CORBEN — W.V.D. HUGHES proceeded to England. Company practising their films for schemes to establish in billets.	

Army Form C. 2118.

18th Battalion
East Surrey Regiment 140th Inf Bde
40th Division

WAR DIARY

or

INTELLIGENCE SUMMARY.

(Erase heading not required.)

VOLUME XVIII

Instructions regarding War Diaries and Intelligence
Summaries are contained in F. S. Regs., Part II.
and the Staff Manual respectively. Title pages
will be prepared in manuscript.

Place	Date	Hour	Summary of Events and Information	Remarks and references to Appendices
GRENAS	4/11/17		Church Parade in the morning	A.1/15
	5/11/17		Battalion billeted at HARLOT. In the morning C + D Coys practised an attack on a village. D Coy attacking & C Coy defending. Olympic GRENAS. Capt A.B. BURTON posted on 14 days leave to England	A.2/15
	6/11/17		In the morning Bn carried out a tactical scheme as allotted area. Night Operations at 5 p.m. Bn attack from a slope line	A.3/15
	7/11/17		In the morning the Bn practised an attack on the village of GRENAS. A, B + C Coys in echelon attacking, D Coy under the senior Regiment of each company defending. Detachment from each company etc. C.S.M. NIGHTINGALE Bn in echelon etc. etc. were selected by Capt. T.R. TUCKER. All etc.	A.4/15

Army Form C. 2118.

WAR DIARY
or
INTELLIGENCE SUMMARY.

(Erase heading not required.)

VOLUME _XVIII_

13 th Battalion.
East Surrey Regiment
120 th Inf. Bde INTELLIGENCE SUMMARY.
40 th Division

Instructions regarding War Diaries and Intelligence
Summaries are contained in F. S. Regs., Part II.
and the Staff Manual respectively. Title pages
will be prepared in manuscript.

Place	Date	Hour	Summary of Events and Information	Remarks and references to Appendices
GREN AS	8/11/17		In the morning, Companies had a Compy training on C Compy HYATZIDE farm. Special training under Specialist Officers in the afternoon.	AP(1) /4
	9/11/17		Battalion was inoculated. A & B Coys moved out to attach to the training according to a previously arranged scheme.	AP(2) /4
	10/11/17		Companies at the disposal of O's C Companies. Inspection of kit, clean Rifles, Box Respirators etc. Lieut E M JAMES proceeds to England for one interview with reference to the future for a transfer to the Indian Army	AP(3) /4
	11/11/17		Two Companies on the range in the morning. Inspection in Billets.	Good
	12/11/17		Training in mood.	[illegible]

A 5834 Wt. W4973/M687 750,000 8/16 D. D. & L. Ltd. Forms/C.2118/13.

13th BATTALION
EAST SURREY REGIMENT   VOLUME XVIII

Army Form C. 2118.

WAR DIARY
or
INTELLIGENCE SUMMARY.

(Erase heading not required.)

120th BRIGADE
40th DIVISION

Instructions regarding War Diaries and Intelligence
Summaries are contained in F. S. Regs., Part II.
and the Staff Manual respectively. Title pages
will be prepared in manuscript.

Place	Date	Hour	Summary of Events and Information	Remarks and references to Appendices
GRÉNAS	13.11.17.		Training of Companies in the HURIÉZBSE FARM area according to the Battalion Scheme.	[signature]
	14.11.17.		Tactical exercise according to Brigade scheme. The 120th Bde. formed the advance guard to the Division advancing via ORVILLE — HALLOY — LOCHUEL — LES CAUMONTS FARM (the 1st Objective) The Bn was in Brigade reserve. n.T.19.c.	[signature]
	15.11.17.		In the morning, Companies training in Outposts.	[signature]
	16.11.17.		The Battalion marched to billets in BERNÉVILLE via POMMERA, BEAUVAL and BEAUMETZ-LES-LOGES.	[signature]

13th BATTALION
EAST SURREY REGIMENT   VOLUME XVIII

WAR DIARY
or
INTELLIGENCE SUMMARY.

(Erase heading not required.)

Instructions regarding War Diaries and Intelligence
Summaries are contained in F. S. Regs., Part II. 120.4 BRIGADE
and the Staff Manual respectively. Title pages 40th DIVISION
will be prepared in manuscript.

Place	Date	Hour	Summary of Events and Information	Remarks and references to Appendices
BEAUVILLE	17.11.17		The Battalion marched into huts at COURCELLES-LE-COMTE via RIVIÈRE, RANSART and ADINFER.	*[initials]*
COURCELLES-LE-COMTE	18.11.17		Parades according to Company arrangements. Training notes issued to Heads of Battalion in Trainers	*[initials]*
	19.11.17	At 6 p.m.	the Battalion left COURCELLES and marched to "A" Camp BEAULENCOURT, via ACHIET-LE-GRAND and BAPAUME	*[initials]*
BEAULEN-COURT	20.11.17		Preparations completed for Emplanes. The known Armoured part of IV Corps from VI Corps.	*[initials]*
	21.11.17		The Battalion marched at 4 a.m. via VILLERS-AU-FLOS, HAPLINCOURT to LEBUCQUIÈRE and were billeted in tents	*[initials]*
	22.11.17		Work. Company arrangements	*[initials]*

A8834. Wt: W4973 M687. 750,000 8/16. D. D. & L. Ltd. Forms/C.2118/13.

13th. BATTALION
EAST SURREY REGIMENT   WAR DIARY   VOLUME XVIII   Army Form C. 2118.
120th BRIGADE   or
40th DIVISION   INTELLIGENCE SUMMARY.

Instructions regarding War Diaries and Intelligence
Summaries are contained in F. S. Regs., Part II.
and the Staff Manual respectively. Title pages
will be prepared in manuscript.

(Erase heading not required.)

Place	Date	Hour	Summary of Events and Information	Remarks and references to Appendices
LEBUCQUIERE	23.11.17		At 4 a.m. the Battalion marched via DEMICOURT and crossed the CANAL DU NORD and arrived with the HINDENBURG SUPPORT line, with BN HQ at K.17.c.5.6.	
	24.11.17		The Battalion moved to the HINDENBURG SUPPORT LINE in K.10. The Commanding Officer proceeded in the evening to 121 Brigade Headquarters at GRAINCOURT CHURCH	
BOURLON WOOD	24–27 11.17.		The Battalion took part in the operations in N.W. End of BOURLON WOOD at BOURLON. For particulars attached hereto despatch of Lt Col H.E. Winder commanding 13th Battn E. Surrey Regt. Casualties Officers killed: Lieut C.I. Hutchison Wounded 2nd Lieut F.G. Wheatcroft Wounded 1 Lieut P.G. de Beauvepaire 1/5th Wounded 1 Lieut R.H. Harris Missing 1 Lieut F.W. Lenham O.R. Killed 31 Acc Wounded 4 Wounded 111 Missing 71	

A5834   Wt. W4973 M687 750,000 8/16   D. D. & L. Ltd   Forms/C.2118/13.

Army Form C. 2118.

WAR DIARY
or
INTELLIGENCE SUMMARY.

(Erase heading not required.)

13th BATTALION
EAST SURREY REGIMENT 120th BRIGADE
40th DIVISION

VOLUME XVIII

Instructions regarding War Diaries and Intelligence Summaries are contained in F. S. Regs. Part II. and the Staff Manual respectively. Title pages will be prepared in manuscript.

Place	Date	Hour	Summary of Events and Information	Remarks and references to Appendices
	28.11.		The Battalion moved from HINDENBURG SUPPORT LINE in K.10. and marched via HARINCOURT, TRESCAULT and METZ; thence by lorry to BAPAUME thence by bus to BLAIRVILLE in the BASSEUX area. Division became part of J.El Corps from IV Corps.	[initials]
	29.11.		Conference employed in refitting etc. according to Battalion arrangements	[initials]
	30.11.		Bath received when the held in ordance from on at 8 hours return. Arrangements as to refitting completed.	[initials]

N. Warden

[signature]
Comdg. 13th Bn East Surrey Regiment

A9834. Wt. W.4973 M687. 750,000. 8/16. D. D. & L. Ltd. Forms/C.2118/13.

Headquarters,

120th Infantry Brigade.

I have the honour to furnish the following report upon the operations of the last few days in so far as these were under my command.

On the 24th November 1917, at about 9:15 p.m., I was ordered to report for orders to G.O.C. 121st Infantry Brigade, and did so at GRAINCOURT. I was informed that the 14th H.L.I. had that day pushed through BOURLON VILLAGE, and were occupying a small portion of the railway line, including the Railway Station, in F. 1.c. and the trench running eastwards from that point to about F.6.Central. I was also informed that the 119th Brigade were holding the N. edge of BOURLON WOOD on the East side. My orders were to clear the western portion of BOURLON VILLAGE of any enemy parties holding out there, to prolong the H.L.I. line on the N. of the Village to the left, and endeavour to continue that line so as to hold the N.W., W., and S.W. outskirts of the Village. To assist in clearing the Village, I was informed I should have the assistance of tanks if possible. There was to be no Artillery barrage. During the evening and night of 24th November, I personally reconnoitred the position, formulated my Scheme for the clearing and holding of the Village, and selected a position of assembly and recon-
:noitred routes. I understood that the Headquarters 14th H.L.I. were somewhere about F.12.d., but was in-
:formed about midnight by the O.s C. 12th Suffolks and 20th Middlesex that it was impossible to reach those Headquarters in safety. I decided that the best method of assisting the H.L.I. and of securing the ground in front

front of BOURLON VILLAGE was first to strengthen the
front line held by the H.L.I., (which I resolved to
do under cover of darkness), and secondly to mop up
the Village with the remainder of my Battalion.   I
assembled the Battalion in the sunk road in E.18.c.,
and explained the scheme to my Company Commanders,
after which I led the Battalion to the position of
assembly in front of the Village.   The position of
assembly extended from about E.12.c.9.2. to E.12.
d.7.7.   By 6 a.m. on the 25th, my Battalion was in
formation on that line.   My scheme had three Com-
:panies in line, each being allotted a definite
sector of the Village and a definite frontage.   The
leading platoon of each Company was to go straight
through the Village in darkness, and join the H.L.I.
in the trench in front, Company Commanders being
instructed to prolong the line as ordered, to consol-
:idate as far as possible, and to distribute in depth.
The remaining three platoons of each of the three
Companies were to mop up the Village in the vicinity
of three different distances from the position of
attack, and each to remain within their own Company
sectors.   My fourth Company was held in reserve on
the N.W. fringe of BOURLON WOOD, with orders to pro-
:tect against any flank attack from the N.W. or W.
During the night 24th/25th, all the roads S. and W.
of BOURLON WOOD were subjected to heavy barrage fire,
but the Battalion had suffered very few casualties
when it formed up for the attack, and by 6 a.m. the
situation was quieter.

I had fixed Zero hour for 6.15 a.m.   No
Tanks had arrived, but as my orders were not condit-
:ional upon the arrival of Tanks, I ordered the
operation to proceed at Zero.   At 6.15 a.m. the
advance/

advance accordingly commenced.   My Headquarters per:
:sonnel had been left in the Quarry at F.24.c. (where
12th Suffolks and 20th Middlesex H.Q.s were).   A few
minutes after the attack had commenced, I found 14th
H.L.I. Bn. H.Q. and handed to Lieut.- Col. Battye the
written message of G.O.C. 121st Infantry Brigade dated
10:25 p.m. 24th, of which message I had been the
bearer. .I explained to Lieut-Col. Battye the scheme
upon which my Battalion was operating, and it met with
his approval.   At about 5.30 a.m., heavy machine gun
fire opened from the N., E., and S. of the house
occupied by Lieut-Col. Battye and myself at F.12.d.5.5.
It was then obvious that strong enemy parties were in
possession of the Northeastern portion of BOURLON WOOD.
With Lieut-Col. Battye's approval, and as there were no
signs of an attack from the West flank, I ordered my
reserve company to proceed southwards and eastwards
through the Wood, and cut off or drive in the enemy
parties operating from the South.   At the same time,
                        clearing
I found that my Right/company had not been able to
make progress through the right of the Village, and I
was able to withdraw most of them, and ordered them to
occupy a position from Battalion H.Q. southeastwards
along a path in the Wood, and to endeavour to obtain
touch with any friendly troops holding a line through
the right of the Wood.   Those two Companies, aided by
the reserve company 14th H.L.I. and by 14th H.L.I.
Headquarters personnel, repelled the attack from the
South, but no information was available as to the posi-
:tion of the 119th Brigade.

        At 7.15 a.m., Lieut-Col. Battye told me he was
wounded.   I had him at once attended to by the M.O.
14th H.L.I., but Col. Battye died within five minutes
after/

after being wounded. I then assumed command of the
situation.

At 7.45 a.m., I received orders (addressed
to O.C. 14th H.L.I.) from G.O.C. 121st Brigade to
capture the Railway line in F.1.c. and d. At that
time, two of my companies were closely engaged fight-
:ing in the Village, and I examined the situation to
see whether any portion of my two other Companies or
of the Company of H.L.I. could be spared to capture
the Railway line. By that time it was obvious that
the enemy held the Village in great strength, and I
found that no sufficient number of troops could be
spared for any further operations through the Village,
having in view the extreme importance of at least
holding the high spur in BOURLON WOOD itself. I was
then about to endeavour to join up my line in the
Wood with the 119th Brigade, when, at 7.50 a.m., the
enemy advanced in force from the E., attacking Bn. H.Q.
and the spur in the Wood. The building occupied as
Battalion H.Q. was in reality North of the Outpost line
I had decided to hold, but as at the time the enemy
could probably not afford to shell it, I decided to
make it a strong point as it held a commanding position
and could be fortified more quickly than a strong point
could be dug in the Wood. I accordingly at once had
the eastern side of the building loopholed and manned,
and I afterwards loopholed a portion of the southern
side of the building and posted snipers in the upper
parts of the house to fire through gaps in the tiles.
The enemy attack was met by Rifle and Lewis Gun fire
from the Companies in the Wood and from Battalion H.Q.
and was ultimately driven off at 8.45 a.m. with con-
:siderable loss to the enemy.

During the day, several enemy parties recon-
:noitring/

reconnoitring the spur in the Wood were dispersed by
fire, and the Strong Point was further strengthened.
Several efforts were also made to push through the
Village, two platoons of my reserve company being at
10.40 a.m. ordered to support the attack through the
Village on the left, but they found it impossible to
make progress or to obtain any touch with the front
line.   They were accordingly withdrawn, and along with
small parties of the attacking companies who had been
driven back, utilised for the further establishing of
an Outpost line to guard the Spur and N.W. edge of the
Wood.   In the early afternoon, I obtained touch with
a representative of O.C. 12th South Wales Borderers,
and ascertained from him that the front line held by
119th Brigade ran from F.14.a.5.3 to F.7.d.5.1, and
slightly Northwards to E.13.d.3.3.   I was informed
that that Brigade was held up by a Strong Point about
F.7.d.3.4.   I accordingly joined up with the Right
Brigade by continuing their Outpost line along roads
to E.12.d.5.6, E.12.d.3.5, E.12.d.4.3, and thence
to the West edge of the Wood, with a refused flank to
the West.   I also proceeded to organise that defence
in depth, and to dig in with entrenching tools, which
were the only available.   I also gave orders for small
patrols to endeavour during the darkness to capture
hostile machine guns which were keeping up an almost
continuous fire on Battalion H.Q. and on the Spur in
the Wood, and gave written orders that the Outpost Line
was to be held at all costs.   At about 3 p.m. on the
25th, the O.C. a party of 14th A. & S.H. in BOURLON
WOOD called and informed me that the Hussars on his right
had withdrawn and left his right flank in the air, his
line being about E.18.b.95.50 to E.18.a.95.50, and he
asked instructions.   I informed him of the situation
and instructed him to hold on, and to bend his right

flank slightly southwards.   Later in the day, an officer
of 121st T.M.B. arrived with two mortars, and after I
had provided a carrying party to bring up ammunition
from the Quarry, those mortars were repeatedly used to
disperse enemy parties and to fire at houses which were
seen to be occupied by machine gunners and snipers.   They
made an appreciable difference in subduing the enemy
fire.

Shortly before dusk, the enemy began to use
Minenwerfer, but as it was too dark to enable him to
range on Battalion H.Q. I resolved to remain there for
the night, and in addition to my Outpost line behind
Battalion H.Q. I put out a series of posts in front.
Enemy snipers had all day been busy from houses and trees
and from the reports I obtained from the attacking Com-
:panies, I learned that the Village was held much too
strongly to justify my making an attack with the troops
at my disposal.

In order to ensure my left flank, I sent at
12.50 p.m. on the 25th, a written message to O.C. 12th
Suffolk Regt. and O.C. 20th Middlesex Regt. (whose
H.Q. were together in the Quarry) asking them for a joint
report of their detailed dispositions, and to pass the
Memo to O.C. 11th King's Own R.L. Regt. (whose H.Q.
were also at the Quarry) for similar information from
him.   To that Memo no reply was ever received.   It was
difficult for runners to move about.

In the evening I received the G.O.C.'s message
dated 2.40 p.m. stating that the Division was being
relieved that night: that Tanks had been ordered up, but
how many or when they would arrive was not known: and
that the Tanks would be used to facilitate the withdrawal
of the H.L.I. Coys. North of the Village and of any
detachments still fighting in the Village.   Completion
of/

of withdrawal was to be reported as early as possible o

Brigade H.Q., and upon that report being received, relief

was to begin.   The Tanks did not arrive that night.   At

8.30 a.m. on the 26th, I sent a written message to the

Officer i/c Tanks, and a small party to find them, but

no Tanks could be found.   At 10.40 a.m. 26th, I informed

Bde. H.Q. by message that the relief could not proceed

as the Tanks had not arrived, and asked for orders.   I

also informed them that hostile aeroplanes were flying

low over the Village and Wood.   My message of 10.40 am

to 121st Brigade H.Q. was delivered by relay runner, and

my Signalling Officer informed me that H.Q. 121st Bde.

had moved from GRAINCOURT, and that H.Q. 107th Bde. who

were then there, refused the Memo and referred the runner

to his own Brigade.   My Signalling Officer accordingly

proceeded to HAVRINCOURT to explain the situation.

In the course of the day, 26th, the enemy

shewed repeated signs of attacking, and in the afternoon

registered Battalion H.Q. with Minenwerfer.   As the

house was not sufficiently strong to resist these, I

resolved to move Battalion H.Q., but it was impossible

to do so until dark on account of the heavy rifle and

machine gun fire all round.   At about 5 p.m. I commenced

the withdrawal of Battalion Headquarters personnel, both

13th West Surreys and 14th H.L.I.   The men were

dribbled back to the Outpost line in parties of three, and

the operation was effected without loss.   Battalion

H.Q. were then established in a dugout in F.18.b.4.8.

Shortly afterwards, I was informed that the

11th K.O.R.L. (less two Coys) had been relieved on my

left flank by a battalion of K.O.Y.L.I. and that my

Outpost line was in course of being relieved in some

places, by platoons of 2/4th Yorks & Lancs Regt.   I

accordingly at 9.30 p.m. sent a message to Brigade stat-

ing/

stating that except for the extrication of the three
Companies H.L.I. I was then in a position to be relieved
and I asked further orders because the Tanks had not yet
arrived.   During that day, 26th, I had again made
unsuccessful efforts to reach the front line Companies
with rations and water and to establish communication.
~~Two~~ Two H.L.I. runners volunteered to reach the front
Companies through the Village, but failed.   I also sent
an Officer's patrol of H.L.I. round the western side of
the Village to endeavour to gain touch, but they were
stopped by hostile machine gun fire very soon after they
left our lines and had to retire.

Meantime about 7 p.m. same day, the enemy
put down a heavy barrage of Artillery and Machine guns
on my Outpost line.   The S.O.S. signal was sent up by
troops on my left, and the response of our Artillery
was immediate and effective.   The barrage lifted once
or twice to 300 or 400 yards, and returned to the Out-
:post line rolling, and the whole Wood and roads on the
left were heavily shelled.   Anticipating attack, I
ordered two more parrallel trenches to be dug in the
neighbourhood of Battalion Headquarters, facing North
and extending across the Wood within my sector.   These
trenches were dug with entrenching tools under heavy
fire, and were occupied all night, (and were occupied
next day by troops of the 62nd Division when their
attack was held up).   No infantry attack developed.
About 7.40 p.m. the enemy sent up several rockets which
burst into two green lights forming an arch, and about
7.50 p.m. or 8 p.m. the barrage ceased.   During the
remainder of the night, the Outpost line was lightly
shelled, with machine gun fire in addition, and the
sunk roads were barraged with shrapnel and H.E.

About 10.30 p.m., the Adjutant of 2/4th Yorks

& Lancs called and informed me of the proposed attack by
62nd Division next day, and he said he had orders to
guide my men out, so that they should not interfere with
the barrage.   I told him I could take my men out, only
if he accepted responsibility for the Outpost line that
night, and as he was not in a position to accept that
then, it was arranged that the responsibility of the
62nd Division for my Outpost line would commence at 5.30
a.m. next day.   As it was then clear that the 62nd
Division, who were to attack with Tanks, and a barrage,
could extricate the H.L.I. Companies if still there, and
as I could get no orders through, I resolved to withdraw
my men between 5.30 and 6 a.m. and keep them in a dugout
                                           well
until the attacking troops had passed/through, otherwise
my withdrawal would adversely influence attacking troops.
Accordingly between 5.30 and 6 a.m. I assembled all
remaining troops of East Surreys and H.L.I. in H.Q. dugout.
The 62nd Division attack was at 6.20 a.m., and, commencing
at 12 noon 27th, I withdrew all my command in small par-
:ties of ten each, -each under an officer, warrant officer
or serjeant,- to the Hindenburg Support Line which we had
previously occupied.   This withdrawal was conducted under
heavy Artillery and machine gun fire, but as routes had
been selected and ordered, the casualties during withdrawal
were very few.

        The total casualties in my battalion were 6
Officers and 223 O.R.

                                        Lieut-Col.

                        Cmdg. 13th Bn. East Surrey Regiment

29.11.17.

To. Adjutant
B. East Surrey Rgt.

Ref your memo. re casualties
I regret that I cannot give you
any numbers. Besides B Coy
is in the village & I can't
get to them. The casualties
now would amount
to 5 OR.
2 Lt. Wheatcroft is wounded
in the stomach & is in the
village with 2 Lt. Beauchamp

My present strength is
1 Offr (Capt Singh) + 6 OR.
Just arrived
2 Lt. Altman + 31 OR

CE Singhleft
OC B Coy

Adjutant.

Estimated casualty returns
12 o.r.

Present strength.
4 officers 110 o.r.

Attached 2/Lt King + 20 o.r. A Coy

A Tucker
Capt.
OC D Coy

1 pm.

c

121 Inf. Bde.

The Divisional Commander wishes me to inform you that the Corps Commander has expressed his high appreciation of the excellent work done by all ranks.

(Signed) W.E. Charles L. Colonel
General Staff of Division

11/7

O.C. 12th Suffolk R.
13 Stephens R.
37 Essex R.
37 Middlesex R.
121 M.G. Coy.
121 T.M.Bty.
144 Field Coy.
121 Field Ambulance
Northamptonshire Yeomanry.

The Brigade Commander wishes the above communicated to all ranks.

R.M. Matthews
Captain,
Brigade M.O.
121st Infantry Brigade

26/11/7

A Coy seem to have been badly knocked about & have withdrawn. I have collected Lt King & about 20 men under my command.

———

I am now with Capt. Lingo, & Burton on road about F 7 d 3.5. awaiting any orders.

Estimated strength of Company 100 other ranks.

10.25

HMSKneller Capt
OC D Coy

O.C.
13th East Surreys.

1. Can you advise me of the hour
that the lorries for conveyance of men
to Back area — are to report —? If
they report early then the 7·30 Am.
Start will be necessary — if not I
do not propose to move from here
until 10·30 A.m. —

2. My medical officer reports that the
men are not fit to move at
7·30 Am. — men are still coming
in —

3. My T.O. wishes to know if Capt
Beecroft has any orders — for move
of Transport?

27/11/17.

S. H. Sanford, Capt.
Commdg 14 H.L.I.

To / Adjutant
                13th East Surrey Regt.

Attached letter from Capt
Hucker passed for the
information of the C.O.

May permission be given for
the two men therein stated

C. E. Sreap Capt.
OC B Co.

12.10 pm.
26
11
17.

To, O.C. Bourlon Defences.

The verbal instructions given to Capt. Burton are being carried out.

C.C. Singh Capt.
O.C. E6 & HLI outposts

12.10 pm.

26/11/17

Adjutant
13 ESR

O.C. Outposts.

Whilst Lt. Rutherford was here awaiting orders as to relief last night my left flank was relieved by a platoon of the Yorks & Lancs. Since then I have not been able to get in touch with Lt. King or Lt. Molenkamp who were the other officers on this flank.

May I send a couple of men back to the Hindenburg support line in order to see if they have withdrawn to our original position

J.R.H.Hinken Capt-
O.C. D Coy

26.11.17

The strength of the missing party is 2 officers & 60 men

Adjutant
13 E.S.R.

Await reply.

Numbers going into
Action.

	Off.	O.R.
H.Q.	5	64
A	4	139
B	4	132
C	4	135
D	4	132
Totals.	21	602

To   Lt. Col Warden
       Comdg.   East Surrey regiment.

     I find, on enquiry, that the C.R.E. of the 40th Division is at the 62nd Divisional H.Q. in the chateau grounds HAVRINCOURT.

     I explained you were resting your men for the night, & that you would proceed to HAVRINCOURT tomorrow: the C.R.E. 40th Div. is arranging accomodation, rations &c for you & your men, also making the necessary arrangements for you to join the 40th Division.

W.H.Brown

Lt. Col. Comdg
178 Bde to I.F.

27.11.17.
At Hermies, 5 limber loads of S.A.A
5 limbers (E.S) full of eqp: on road to HAVRINcourt.
1 Cooker   "   "   "   "
1 water Cart   -   -   -   -
Animals for limbers, but not for Cooker & water Carts.
No forage=
Wants 4 H.D. horses to bring to Havrincourt.

Joe

13th East Dorsets

No word as to arrangements
for lorries to convey men to Back
area has been received. –
62nd Div. were to let us know
time & place of rendezvous. – I
am therefore not moving until
10-30 a.m. this morning or such
other time as may fit in with
orders received from Div

28/11/7

Shackleford Capt
Comdg 14th E.D.

20

13th February

13th. Bn. East Surrey Regt.

Casualties.

Other Ranks.

Killed.	32.
Died of Wounds.	5.
Wounded & Missing	23.
Missing (believed killed).	1.
Missing.	54.
Wounded.	108.
	228.

Officers.

Killed (Capt Lowe)	1
Died of Wounds (Lieut Wheatcroft)	1.
Wounded & Missing (Lieut Harter)	1.
Missing (Lieut Graham)	1.
Wounded (Lieut Beauchamp)	1.
	5.

To

Adjutant,
13th East Surrey Rgt.

Up to the present I have
not been able to get
the Coy Commander of Y & L.
I am in touch with the
senior Subalton & urgent
messages have been sent
for the Coy Commander.
The Subalton states
that he cannot get the
over the outposts.

C.E. Linge Capt.
OC outposts

MESSAGES AND SIGNALS.

Prefix .... Code .... m.	Words	Charge	This message is on a/c of :	Recd. at .... m.
Office of Origin and Service Instructions.				Date ....
....	Sent		.... Service.	From ....
....	At .... m.			
....	To			
....	By		(Signature of "Franking Officer.")	By ....

TO { Lt Col Battye — Comdg. 14ᵗ H.L.I.

	Sender's Number.	Day of Month.	In reply to Number.	A A A
*		24ᵗ		

13ᵗ East Surrey Regt and 11ᵗ
Kings Own (less 2 companies attached
to 119ᵗ Bde) are proceeding to cooperate
with you in holding BOURLON VILLAGE
You will take command of
the above troops and~~lot~~ any ~~they~~
~~Batn~~ of my 12ᵗ Suff. or 25ᵗ Midd who
may be in or in the vicinity of BOURLON.
My 12ᵗ Suffolks and 25ᵗ Midd. are
dead beat. The following dispositions
are suggested but my information
is not very clear therefore you will
take the action you consider most
suitable.

13ᵗ E. Surrey Regt. to prolong your left
particular attention should be
paid to securing the left flank (Way

From				
Place				
Time				

The above may be forwarded as now corrected.   (Z)

....

Censor.   Signature of Addressor or person authorised to telegraph in his name.

* This line should be erased if not required.

750,000. W 2186—M509. H. W. & V., Ld. 6/16.

Army Form C.2121
(in pads of 100).
No. of Message _____

Prefix _____ Code _____ m.	Words	Charge	This message is on a/c of:	Recd. at _____ m.
Office of Origin and Service Instructions.				Date _____
_____	Sent		_____ Service.	
_____	At _____ m.			From _____
_____	To _____			
_____	By _____		(Signature of " Franking Officer.")	By _____

| TO | | | | |

| Sender's Number. | Day of Month. | In reply to Number. | |
| * | | | **A A A** |

of the village. Your message regarding occupation of cellars by enemy just received, have asked Division to send Tanks if possible to assist in the morning. Divne Comdr. wishes village held at all costs. ~~He required~~ Suggest 12ᵗʰ ?uff + 20ᵗʰ Midd form composite Batn to hold spur E.17b 18a to which I attach great importance. Understand S.W.B. of 119ᵗʰ Bde. are holding road N. edge of village through F.7.a.

John Campbell
B.G.

10-25 p.m.

From

Place 24-11-17

Time

The above may be forwarded as now corrected.

(Z)

Censor. | Signature of Addressor or person authorised to telegraph in his name.

* This line should be erased if not required.

750,000. W 2186—M509. H. W. & V., Ld. 6/16.

Adjutant.

Disposition report
despatched 10·25.

Immediately Lt King
withdrew from the village
I ~~spoke~~ suggested leading
A Coy some men.
King was of the opinion
that only more casualties
would be the result

of sending men into
the village. He states
that the enemy have
machine guns in 2
broken down tanks
& that progress is
not possible.

                    M Dunbar
                         Capt
                    O C D Coy

10.50
26/11/17

From 121 Bde. HQ

To, OC. 13th E. Surreys.

I was ordered to bring these
orders verbally to you from
121 Bde Hqr & guide Col
Maitland up here to you fetching
up guides at the quarry.
There are no guides who
know where your Battn Hq
are now & so I leave these
orders with Col Maitlands
note.

orders from Bde as follows:—
OC. E. Surreys is Commanding
E. Surreys. H.L.I & Kings Own
troops in the wood area
Col. Maitland, with 4th Y & L

as soon as you are in position —

7. You will use the troops at your
disposal to clear the villages of
the enemy, remembering this is
a secondary operation particularly
as regards use of tanks —

8. I am moving a dismounted
carp. regt. to the sunken road
E.23.b. 24 a. to relieve any
troops of 21. Middx R. there and
am ordering them (21. Middx) to
move forward on to spur in
E.17 b. 18 a and thus ~~to set~~ Fresh
enable you to withdraw any troops
you have there should you require
them — You will not use troops of
my Brigade as they are not fit
for more —

John Campbell
B.G.
Comdg 121 Bde

25-11-17.
B.G.

O.C. 14th H.L.I.

<u>Secret.</u>

1. In order to enable cavalry to get forward ~~tomorrow~~ today 25th it is necessary to capture the railway line in F.1. c and d.

2. You will be prepared to carry out this operation with the troops at your disposal at an hour to be notified later. Infantry will not go further than 100 yards in front of the railway as arty. may be required to search the ground in that direction –

3. I understand from your report that you hold most of the railway indicated, if not and you can advance and hold it do so once there is no objection to unit of 119th

Brigade on your ~~left~~ moving forward
to cooperate.

4. 12 Tanks are placed at your
disposal and arrive in BOURLON
village at 6 a.m. these are
intended to assist in gaining
the line of the railway which
is of paramount importance.
If it is necessary however you
may at your discretion detach
two to cooperate with you in
clearing up village —

5. Arrangements have been made
for field artillery to fire intermittent
rolling barrage in F. 2. a. F. 1. b. and a
and E 6. b.

6. Probable hour of attack to gain
railway 9 a.m. as it may not be
possible to notify you in time of
the hour you should endeavour
to occupy your objectives along
railway by 9 a.m. and report as

To

Adjutant
13th East Surreys

Will you please inform me where the Bn is to move to. Relieving troops are taking over now.

12.10 AM. E Showerlow

Od 13

26/11/17

plus 2 Coys 5ᵗʰ KOYLI. is
relieving all troops of 121 & 120
Bde who are in the line

The Col of Kings Own Bn, in
the Quarry just off Cambrai Rᵈ
wants to know if you have
any orders as to where he
is to go when relieved.

~~the B.M. of 121 Bde very~~
~~kindly sent the telegram~~
~~if I can get any more men~~
~~approx. strength of~~
~~all~~ (Scot)

Col Maitland wants you to
hand over all tools, and
all Lewis gun drums if

Capt.
13th - E. Surrey Regt.

Position now becoming more satisfactory.
Shelling decreasing in intensity.
Few direct hits on road, which
is quite the best position the men
could be in.
Have had some more casualties,
mostly wounded.
Mr. Dickson of H.L.I. did not go
to get into touch with other Coys,
of H.L.I. of whom I have no news.
All my officers are all right.

A B Brenton
Capt.
O.C. C Coy
13" E. S. Regt.

9.40 P.M.
By Runner.
26/11/17

Capt.
13th E. Surrey Regt.

Duplicate

Adjutant.
13th East Surrey Rgt

Am in communication with
187th Brigade, who took over
from 124 Brigade

3 Batt Hdqrs are at the
Sugar Refinery E29A and
communication to brigade can
be got with that post.

Louis W. Pinnock
Lieut
Signals Officer
13th E.S.R

Nov 26/17
11.50 AM   E30 C central

When the battalion is relieved will
you please send a message addressed
to each relay post telling them to
close down and where to report.

Aylmer
13th E.S.R.

To Adjutant
13th East Surrey Regt

Attached returned to you
The Orders therein are
being put into execution
now

L. C. Emery Capt
5.20 pm   13th East Surrey Regt

25
—
11
/17   By Runner

To Adjutant
13th East Surrey Rgt

We are holding (C Coy ESR
C Coy HLI)+ 1 Platoon B Coy)
The same positions.
Very lights are coming
from same position.
Casualties about 15 - 20.
Situation almost normal
2 Runners from a
Brigadier wanted $

know whether we knew
anything about the 3 Corps
of H.L.I. The name of
the Brigadier is not
known.

C.C. Sings Capt
OC B Coy

7.45 p.m.

26
/
11
/
15

Adjutant.
13th East Surrey Rgt.

Am in communication with
187th Brigade, who took over
from 121st Brigade.
  3 Batt H.Qs are at the
Sucrere Sugar Refinery E 29 A
& communication by brigade can be got with
that post.

Louis W. Pinnick
Lieut
Signals Officer
13th E.S R

Nov 26 17

E 30 C central

S.W.B

12ᵗ ~~Welch~~ Regt. whose H.R. are at
dug out ANNEUX CHAPEL F.19.C.2.9
from whom situation in wood can
be obtained.

6. Give bearer, Lt Aitken, 6ᵗ D.9.
any assistance or information
he may require.

7. The Object to be kept in view is to
ensure a practicable gap for
the Cavalry across the railway
F.1.C. + d.

John Lamphrey
S.9.

25-11-17

9.20 am

O.C. 13th E. Surrey Regt.

Ref: your memo 7-40 a.m.

1. You will now be in command in the vicinity of BOURLON.

2. The whole of BOURLON WOOD is held by 119th Bde. and is secure. Any m.g. fire from the East is from beyond the edge of wood.

3. You will ensure that the Village is cleared thoroughly and made defensible particularly on West flank. Infy. should be some 200 yds outside hut advantage should be taken of existing enemy trenches.

4. Ensure that the railway F.1.C.+d is occupied and the enemy driven down slope to the north.

5. Gain touch with Lt Col. Benzie comdg

& I am now with 5th
Beaumont with 2 Platoons
of C Coy & we are
attempting to make a
flank attack through
Bourlon Wood.
Capt Lowe & 2 Lt Wheatcroft
are wounded

C E Lings Capt
OC B Coy

10h 57
25
11
/

To Adjutant
13th East Surrey Regt

I have tried to rejoin my
Coy in village but it
is impossible. I am
now with Capt Burtt
in sunken road in
Bourlon Wood with
5 men (7.y.d.7.3.)

10.57 AM.
25
II
17

E. Linglight
2 Lieut

To Adjutant

13ᵗʰ East Riding Reg

I sent the following to you
at 7.45 AM ~~~~~ to day

B Coy held up in the
village E 12. A. 7. 0. Coy is
very badly cut up. It
is impossible to get
reinforcements to them.
Enemy HQ 2ⁿᵈ were
forced to with draw

Adjutant,

Will you please inform me whether you require the 2 platoons that are guarding C Coy's rear on the North Western edge of the wood to report to you.

J.W. Hacker Capt.
OC D Coy

1 pm

To Lt Col Warden
                    15th East Surrey Regt
OC Boulon Defences.

East Surrey & H.L.I. outposts
in positions as laid down
in orders issued at 5·20 pm
Connection is maintained with
119th Inf Bde outposts on the
right.
12th S.W.B's are holding sunken
Suffolks
road at E·12·c·2·5 on left

                    C.E. Singe Capt
                    OC E.S.R & H.L.I
                    Outposts

6·45 pm
25
___
11
___
11   By Runner
      2865? Pte Hemstock.

Aaf. 13ᵗᵉ ~~Survey~~ Regt.

① Estimated casualties

Wounded O.R. 10

Killed Officers 1

O.R. 6

Officer killed 2/Lt C. I. HENDERSON

② Actually present 88 O.R.

3 Officers

1.30 P.M.
25/11/17

A B Bretton
Capt
OC Coy

O.C.

B   Lt P. Ralph

C   2/Lt E. Capt

D   2/Lt Hope

1. Please let me have casualty (estimated) Return.

2. At the same time give me actually numbers of your present strength.

3. Am I justified in to approve &c d be given by name.

4. The C.O. would like to see 2/Lt Parker of "C" Coy

12.25 pm
25/11/17.

Dainty
Capt & adj.

Adjutant

13ᵗʰ East Surreys.

The enclosed was handed
to me at 9.15.

Since then I have been
trying to get into touch with
the C.O. & the other Coy. Cmders.

The position of my
Company is as follows

2 platoons in trenches
at E 18 a 9.9

2 platoons in BOURLON
WOOD about E 18 b 8.5

The Commanding Officer
13th East Surreys.

The C.O. of the 4th Yr L Regt.
called here this evening
& lacking information as to
the whereabouts of BHQ left
attached note to be forwarded.

Apparently 3 platoons of his
Bn. are relieving our 2 companies
in the front line & another platoon
the Bn on our right. I am
requested to pass the first platoon
accordingly along our Bn. front
(from Pltn. cdr. to Pltn. cdr.) for the
latter purpose.

I have sent 1 guide to meet
the incoming Company so it
will only be necessary to send
two more.

R W Hyam ?Lieut.

a Coy.

of tanks

8. I am moving a dismounted
Cav. regt. to the Sunken road
E 23.b. 2.4.a to relieve any
troops of 21st Middx there and
am sending them (21st Middx)
to move forward on to spur
in E 17 & 18 a and thus for
enable you to withdraw any
fresh troops you have there
shd you require them. You will
not use troops of my Bde as
they are not fit for more —

John Campbell
B.G.

6.38 a.m.
25-11-17

at 6 a.m. These are intended
to assist in gaining the line
of the railway which is of paramount
importance. If it is necessary
however you may at your
discretion detail two to cooperate
with you in clearing up village.

5. Arrangements have been
made for F.A. to fire in Knuitk____
sling Farmage in 7.2a - 7.1.b
and a area E.6.b.

6. Probable hour of attack to gain
railway 9 a.m. As it may not be
possible to notify you of the hour
you shd. endeavour to occupy
your objective along railway
by 9 a.m. and report as
soon as you are in position.

7. You will use the troops at your
disposal to clear the village
of the enemy remembering
this is a secondary operation
particularly as regards us

U.C. 14.:-H.L.1.

1. In order to enable cavalry to get forward today 25th it is necessary to capture the railway line in 7.1 c + d.

2. You will be prepared to carry out this operation with the troops at your disposal at an hour to be notified later. Infantry will not go further than 400 yds in front of the railway as arty may be reqd. to search the grnd in that direction.

3. I understand from your reports that you hold most of the railway indicated, if not & you can advance & hold it do so now. There is no objection to use of 119th Bde on your right moving forward to cooperate.

4. 12 Tanks are placed at your disposal & arriving in BOURLON VILL

O.C. 13 East Surrey R.R.

I have been unable to find your Batt'n H.Q. & your left Coy cannot direct me —

I am going to relieve you in the front line from E.18a 5.9 to E.12d 8.5 tonight 25/26 inst with one company —

Will you please send 3 guides (one for each platoon) to the QUARRY at E.24c 7.8 as soon as possible to guide this company in —

A.E. Maitland
Lt Col
2/4 York & Lancs.

in Bourlon Wood about E.18. 6. 5. 0.
I am going on to reconnoitre, and
will meet battalion at the position of
assembly.

The battalion is to start at
11 p.m. tonight.

Bombs, S.A.A, Rations, Lewis Guns
&c to be carried.

Packs can be dumped if desired
by Coy Cmdrs & left under guard, but
rations must be brought, & iron
rations and water.

H.J. Warden
Lieut Col.
24. 10. 17.
Cmdg: 13th Bn E. Surry.

Dump my pack, but bring my
socks and wool Jerkin — also my
field glass.
H.J.W.

Adjutant
13th Bn. East Surrey Regt.

The battalion is under orders of
G.O.C. 121st Inf. Bde. and is to
obtain possession tomorrow morning
of the NW and SW outskirts of
BOURLON VILLAGE.   Please
bring battalion by platoons with intervals
through GRAINCOURT (Cross Roads
will be picketed by 121 Bde.) ——
CAPT. SMEE will meet Bn. at
K.5. a 8.1. and guide to ~~position~~
~~QUARRY at E. 24.0. 6.8.~~

~~guides will meet you at the Quarry~~
~~(from   ) to guide battalion~~
~~to position of assembly at E.18.6.5.0~~
~~in the woods.~~

point on CAMBRAI road about E. 23 d. 5. a.
At that point you will be met by
guides from ~~the~~ 12th Suffolks, who will
guide battalion to position of assembly

5. It is expected that the Divisions are to be relieved tonight, after the front-line troops have been withdrawn under cover of Tanks.

6. The password for the Outposts will be JOHNNY — WALKER, but the password will not be known to friendly troops in rear of the outpost line.

H.J. Warden Lieut Col

Cmdg. BOURLON defenses.

25-10-17.

All O.C. Coys with the exception of A Coy have read these orders

E.C. Single Capt.

point to E.12.d.8.9.   O.C. B
Coy East Surreys will continue the line
along the road to Cross Roads at E.12.d.3.5
and be responsible for the road leading
thence to the Village.   O.C. D Coy. East
Surreys will continue the line along the
road running first southwards and
then southwestwards to E.18.a.9.9, — a
refused flank being formed to the left.

4.   Troops should dig in to obtain some
cover.   If there are too many troops
for a single line, Supports will be
formed.   O.C. Coys should, if annoyed
by machine gun fire during the night, send
out small patrols to capture the hostile
machine Guns.   In the event of the
village being captured by the enemy, the
outpost line in rear is to be held at
all costs.

5.

O's C. Coys.

1. Three Coys. of H.L.I. are holding the trench N. of BOURLON from the Railway line to about E.6.d.3.7. ~~& No 8 and 9 Stations East Surreys now attempt tonight to reinforce the left of the H.L.I. and extend the front to the road at E.6.c.3.2, if possible.~~

2. The remainder of the force will act as outposts, of which Capt. Hinge will be in command as far as regards H.L.I. and East Surreys.

3. The 121st Bde. line in the wood joins at its right with the 119th Bde. line at E.7.d.2.1. On the left it stretches to E.12.d.7.2. O.C. C. Coy, East Surreys, will continue the line from there, along the road, to Bn. Hd. at E.12.d 5.6, and be responsible for guarding with a Lewis Gun & rifles the road from this

will be paid to the security of <u>2</u>.
the left flank —

4. Completion of withdrawal
will be reported as early as
possible to Bde. H.Q.

5. On report in 4 being received
relief will begin of the former.
lin

J Mac Campbell
R.S.

2.40 p.m.
25-11-17.

O.C. E. Surrey Regt.

~~OC 12th Suffolk Reg~~

1. The Division is being relieved tonight.

2. Tanks have been ordered up but how many or when they will arrive is not known.

3. The tanks will be used to ~~withdraw~~ facilitate the withdrawal of the Corps. Hdt. north of the village and of any detachments still fighting in the village. On withdrawal the tanks will cover the consolidation of the defensive line now held round the S.E. S - S.W. fringe of the village. The position on the Spur E 17.6.a. a.b.a. will be further strengthened and touch ensured on the right flank with 119th. Bde. Particular attention

O.C. E Surrey Regt,

You will push forward at once and gain touch with Col. Battye If necessary you will fight your way through the village at the East end and reach the trench in front. This is most urgent and will be carried out without delay. Touch

must be joined with
H.L.I. forthwith.

2. Col. Battye has
orders to occupy
railway in F.1.c & d.
by 9 a.m. 12 tanks
should now be in
the village BOURLON
for this purpose. If
necessary 2 tanks
may be detached

& assist in clearing village.

3. Act at once and gain touch without further delay.

John Murphy
Bg.

7.20 a.m.

25.10.17.

O.C. B Coy. L.S. Col Coph.
C " " " Johnston.
D " " " Pte H Capt.
6 " " H.L.!

      The whole of your respective Companies will be accommodated in the Deep Dug out now occupied by the H.Q of H.L.I & L.S.

      The withdrawal from the present Outpost line will commence at 5.30 am tomorrow morning and all troops of both H.L.I & L.S must be in the Dug out by 6 am.

      The presence of other troops moving up is in order.

      The withdrawal must be in small parties

11. 40 pm
26/11/17

Davies
Capt H.L.I

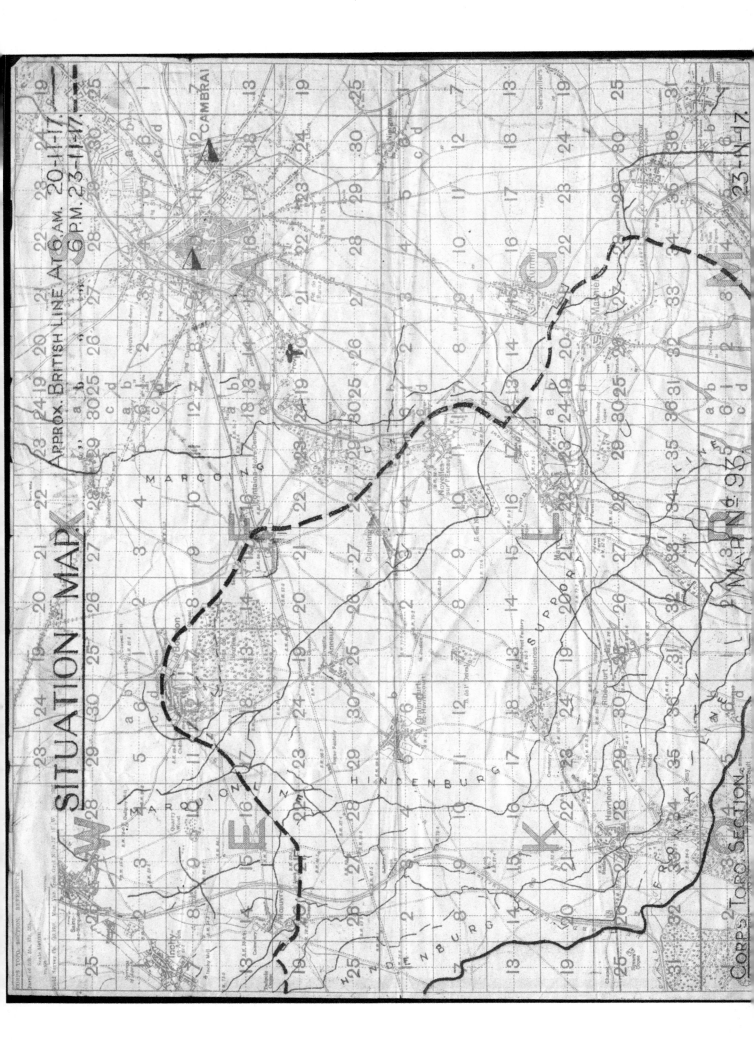

SITUATION MAP.

APPROX. BRITISH LINE AT 6 A.M. 20·11·17. ——
6 P.M. 23·11·17. ▬ ▬ ▬

CAMBRAI

2 CORPS. TOPO SECTION. MAP N°. 6. 95. 23·11·17.

BOURLON VILLAGE.

13th EAST SURREY REGIMENT

DECEMBER 1917.

Vol 19

WAR DIARY

— OF THE —

13TH. BATTN. EAST. SURREY. REGT,

[120TH BRIGADE, 40TH DIVISION],

FOR THE MONTH OF

DECEMBER, 1917.

19 D
10 sheets

Army Form C. 2118.

WAR DIARY

or

INTELLIGENCE SUMMARY.

(Erase heading not required.)

Instructions regarding War Diaries and Intelligence Summaries are contained in F. S. Regs. Part II. and the Staff Manual respectively. Title pages will be prepared in manuscript.

Place	Date	Hour	Summary of Events and Information	Remarks and references to Appendices

A5834 Wt. W4973/M687 750,000 8/16 D. D. & L. Ltd. Forms/C.2118/13.

13TH BATTALION,
EAST SURREY REGIMENT, **WAR DIARY**
or
120TH INF. BRIGADE INTELLIGENCE SUMMARY.
40TH DIVISION.

Instructions regarding War Diaries and Intelligence
Summaries are contained in F. S. Regs., Part II.
and the Staff Manual respectively. Title pages
will be prepared in manuscript.

(Erase heading not required.)

Place	Date	Hour	Summary of Events and Information	Remarks and references to Appendices
BLAIRVILLE [LENS 14 A6]	1.12.'17		Companies at disposal of O.sC. Companies. Refitting and general re-organisation in progress.	W.S. Dott.v/h.
D.º	2.12.17		Church Parade at 11 a.m.	W.S. Dott./h.
ARMAGH CAMP, HAMELINCOURT 3.12.17 (51b.1:40,000)	3.12.17		120th INF. BGDE relieved 49th INF BGDE in Div.l Reserve at HAMELINCOURT. Batt.ⁿ quartered in ARMAGH CAMP; took over from 1/R.D.F. The Batt.ⁿ marched via BLAIRVILLE, FICHEUX, BOISLEUX-AU-MONT to the Camp. Canteen Comm.ᵉᵉ appointed :— MAJOR W.G.T. KEDDIE, M.C.[Pres.t], Lieut.W.G. Price & 2/Lt N.E. Dobb (Members)	W.S.Dott.v/h.
D.º	4.12.17	11 a.m.	C.O.s parade – 10 a.m. Companies under O.sC.Co.ts for Close & Extended order drill and Bayonet fighting from 11 to 1 p.m. Specialists (Sig.ª, Scouts & Snipers, Bombers and L.G.s] under Specialist officers. 4 men per Platoon practised in Rapid Wiring. During afternoon, O.sC.Co.ts, Plat.Comm.ts and Platoon Serg.ts visited places of Assembly under Brigade Defence Scheme.	W.S.(ⱼ) /h.
		5.30p.m.	C.O. lectured to Officers and N.C.O.s on "RAIDS".	/h.
D.º	6.12.17	9a.m.to 11a.m.	Bayonet Fighting for "A" and "B" Co.ts on Assault Course at A106.5.7. "C" and "D" under O.Cs.	W.B.D. /h.
		11a.m.to 1p.m.	Rapid Wiring practice, etc.	
		9.30a.m. to 1 p.m.	Signallers (under Signalling Sgt.); Runners (under Signalling Off.); Bombers & L.G.s under Specialist Off.—	

13th BATTALION,
EAST SURREY REGT., WAR DIARY.

or

INTELLIGENCE SUMMARY.

120th INF. BDE.,
40th DIVISION.

Instructions regarding War Diaries and Intelligence
Summaries are contained in F. S. Regs., Part II.
and the Staff Manual respectively. Title pages
will be prepared in manuscript.

(Erase heading not required.)

Place	Date	Hour	Summary of Events and Information	Remarks and references to Appendices
ARMAGH CAMP, HAMELINCOURT.	5.12.17	2-4.30 p.m.	Afternoon devoted to Sports and Games under Companies' arrangements.	W.E.O. 2/Lt.
		5.30pm.	The C.O. lectured to Officers and N.C.O's on "The New Sector".	
D°.	6.12.17	9a.m.to 1p.m.	Under Col Commanders – Rapid wiring and general C.I. training. "C"Co. Bayonet fighting on Assault Course (11a.m. to 12 noon); "D" Co. from 12 noon to 1 p.m.; L.G's, Bombers (under Specialist Off.); Signallers under Signalling Off.; Runners under Specialist Off.	W. 6. O. 2/Lt.
			Afternoon devoted to Sports and Games.	
			Working party (100 men) at STALEYBRIDGE DUMP – 8 p.m. to 5 a.m. – 7th inst.	
D°.	7.12.17	–	Specialist training as on 6th inst. Companies practised in Musketry.	W.E.O. 2/Lt.
			Working party (100 men) at STALEYBRIDGE DUMP – 8 p.m. to 5 a.m. – 8th inst.	
D°.	8.12.17	9a.m.to 1p.m.	Companies at disposal of O's.C Companies. Rifle Range and Assault Course were utilised.	W.E.O. 2/Lt.
		2.30 to 3.30p.m.	R.G's instructed in use of N° 35 Grenade. Otherwise the afternoon was a half-holiday.	
D°.	9.12.17	10a.m.	Church Parade.	W.E.O. 2/Lt.
			The C.O., 2nd in Command, O's.C Companies, Assist. Adju; and the B.I.O. visited the line to reconnoitre the new Sector.	

A5834 Wt. W4973 M687 750,000 8/16 D. D. & L. Ltd. Forms/C.2118/13.

13TH BATTALION EAST SURREY REGT.,

WAR DIARY

or

INTELLIGENCE SUMMARY

Intelligence 120TH INFANTRY BGDE., 40TH DIVISION.

(Erase heading not required.)

Instructions regarding War Diaries and Intelligence
Summaries are contained in F. S. Regs., Part II.
and the Staff Manual respectively. Title pages
will be prepared in manuscript.

Place	Date	Hour	Summary of Events and Information	Remarks and references to Appendices
FONTAINE-CROISILLES. SECTOR	10. XII. 17		The 120th Brigade relieved the 121st Brigade in FONTAINE-CROISILLES sector. The Batt⁰ (plus 1 Co⁷ 11th Roy. Lancs Reg⁷.—in close support) relieved the 20th Middlesex Reg⁷. (and 1 Co⁷ 21st Midd⁺ Reg⁷) in Left Sub-Sector, Left Sector. Relief was completed by 2 p.m. Batt⁰ H.Q. were established at T.22.d.6.9. Dispositions of Companies: "A" – Rt. Co⁷ "B" – Rt. Centre Co⁷ "C" – Left Centre Co⁷ "D" – Left Co⁷. Patrols went out from Rt. and Left Co⁷ˢ during night but found nothing unusual. Artillery—on both sides—fairly active. Usual work in trenches in progress.	W.B.D. ⅍
Dᵒ.	11. XII. 17.		Patrols went out from Rt. Centre, Left Centre and Left Co⁷ˢ. Our artillery active chiefly on Rt Co⁷ˢ sector. Usual trench work in progress.	W.B.D. ⅍
Dᵒ	12. XII. 17		Enemy barraged our lines between 7 a.m. and 8.15 a.m. Our artillery and M.G's replied. Patrols went out from Left and Left Centre Co⁷ˢ.	W.B.D. ⅍
Dᵒ	13. XII. 17		Enemy artillery quiet until 5.50 p.m. when fairly heavy bombardment commenced and continued until 6.30 p.m. Several enemy gas-shells sent over between 12 noon and 1 p.m. and 10.30 p.m. & midnight. Patrols out from Left, Left Centre and Rt. Centre Co⁷ˢ.	W.B.D. ⅍

A5834 Wt. W4973 M687 739,000 8/16 D. D. & L. Ltd. Forms/C.2118/13.

13TH BATTN EAST SURREY REGT.,
/20TH INF. BGDE,/
40TH DIVISION.

WAR DIARY

or

INTELLIGENCE SUMMARY.

Army Form C. 2118.

Instructions regarding War Diaries and Intelligence
Summaries are contained in F. S. Regs., Part II.
and the Staff Manual respectively. Title pages
will be prepared in manuscript.

(Erase heading not required.)

Place	Date	Hour	Summary of Events and Information	Remarks and references to Appendices
FONTAINE-CROISILLES	14.12.17		Patrols out from both centre Coys during the night. The Battn was relieved by 11th K.O. (Royal Lancs) Regt. and withdrew to "Support" Battn H.Q. established at T.22.d.— "A" Coy withdrew to Sunken Road T.17.a.35; "B" Coy (2 plat. in road T.17.c; 2 plat. in SHAFT AVENUE (Coy H.Q. at 16.a.t.); "C" Coy in posts by platoons — Posts; C.6; C.7; C.8; C.10; Coy H.Q. C.9. "D" Coy remained in close support in SHAFT AVENUE.	W.B.D. 2/Lt. 2/Lt
In Support. —See 14th inst.	15.12.17		Working party found by "A" Coy. for Front line. Fire-steps constructed and general positions improved by "A", "B" & "C" Coys and general work in progress by B.H.Q. personnel. "D" Coy. under 11th K.O.R.L. Regt. All companies "Stood-to" 6.30 a.m. until 9 a.m.	W.B.D. 2/Lt.
Do.	16.12.17		"A" Coy. and "C" Coy. relieved each other. Front line working party found by "C" Coy. "Stand-to"-6.30 a.m. to 8.30 a.m. Work as usual. Lieut. A.W. Gill rejoined battn from 40th Div. Depôt Battn.	W.B.D. 2/Lt. 2/Lt
Do.	17.12.17		Work, etc. as for 16th inst.	
ARMAGH CAMP, 18.12.17 HAMELINCOURT			Battn relieved by 20th Middlesex Regt. and returned in reserve to ARMAGH CAMP HAMELINCOURT (S 23 c 44)	W.B.D. 2/Lt

A.5834. Wt. W4973 M687 730,000 8/16 D. D. & L. Ltd. Forms/C.2118/13.

13TH BATTN EAST SURREY REGT.

WAR DIARY

or

INTELLIGENCE SUMMARY.

(Erase heading not required.)

120TH INF. BGDE,
40TH DIVISION.

Place	Date	Hour	Summary of Events and Information	Remarks and references to Appendices
ARMAGH CAMP, HAMELINCOURT.	19.XII.17	9.30am 7 to 12.30 P.m.	Physical drill; Gas&respirator practice; Squad-drill with and without arms. Afternoon devoted to Sport and games. Working-party 100 men found for work near ECOUST. Lieut. A. W. Morris returned from leave.	W.S.D. 2/A.
Dº	20.XII.17	9a.m.to 12.45 p.m. 2 to 3.30 p.m.	Squad drill without arms; Anti-gas training; Squad-drill with arms; Bombing; Bayonet fighting. L.G's; Signallers and Runners, Rifle G's and Scouts and Snipers under Specialist Officers.	W.S.D. 1/A.
Dº.	21.XII.17		Programme as for 20th plus Ceremonial Drill and practice in saluting	W.S.D. 2/A.
Dº	22.XII.17		The G.O.C. IV Corps attended at CLONMEL CAMP, HAMELINCOURT. The Battⁿ paraded and the following received the riband of the Military Medal awarded them for meritorious conduct in the action at BOURLON WOOD:- Nº 19585, Pte E.F.EVENDEN, 13654, Cpl E.CATLIN, 11957, Pte W.A.WILLS, 16504, Sgt J.DOOLEY, 1672, Pte W.R.DIBBLE, 13442, Pte H.J.THATCHER. 25862 Pte J.EDWARDS, 411, 4/C. J.CHASE, 6737 " H.CASTLE , The undermentioned recipients were not present at the Parade:-	W.S.D. 1/A.

13th EAST SURREY REGIMENT, WAR DIARY

120th INF. BGDE,

or

INTELLIGENCE SUMMARY.

(Erase heading not required.)

Instructions regarding War Diaries and Intelligence
Summaries are contained in F. S. Regs., Part II.
and the Staff Manual respectively. Title pages 40th DIVISION.
will be prepared in manuscript.

Place	Date	Hour	Summary of Events and Information	Remarks and references to Appendices
ARMAGH CAMP, HAMELINCOURT.	22.XII.17		Nº 18376, Pte C. JOHNSTON (On leave); Nº 230, Pte A. BANCE (Wounded 26/11/17); Pte D. SMYTHE (Wounded 11/11/17); Sgt J. BRIGGS (Wounded 26/11/17); Cpl J. KNIGHT (Wounded 14/11/17) and Pte A. W. BROOKER (Wounded 26/4/17). Lieut. W. V. L. MALLETT, Lieut. F. SIMONIS and 2/Lieut H. M. S. BAILEY - all from 5th (R.) Battⁿ E. Surrey Regⁿ joined the Battⁿ and were posted to Companies - "D", "C", "B" respectively.	W.C.D. H.L.
Dº	23.XII.17	10a.m.	Church Parade. O. Cˢ "C" and "D" Coʸˢ, the Adjutant, Lieuts Thompson, Morris, Mallett, Simonis and 2/Lt. Bailey visited the line to reconpoitre.	W.C.D. H.L.
FONTAINE-CROISILLES SECTOR- LEFT BATTⁿ	24.XII. '17		Battⁿ left ARMAGH CAMP and relieved 21st Middx. (121st Bgde) in Left sub-sector of Left sector [FONTAINE-CROISILLES area. Battⁿ H.Q. established at T6b40.; Brigade H.Q. at 121d59.CROISILLES Coʸ Dispositions:— Rt- "C" Coʸ . Left Centre- "A" Coʸ. Rt. Centre- "B", Left Coʸ - "D". 1 Coy 11th R. Lancs in Support [SHAFT AVENUE]. Night Patrols went out from each Coʸˢ front but found nothing unusual. Artillery fairly active. Lieut. Col. H. L. WARDEN proceeded on leave to SCOTLAND. Major W. G. T. KEDDIE in command of Battⁿ. 2/Lt. F. R. WOODWARD returned to duty from Army Signalling School, DUNSTABLE.	[Ref. FONTAINE trench map. W.C.D. H.L.

A5834 Wt W4973 M687 750,000 8/16 D. D. & L. Ltd. Forms/C.2118/13.

WAR DIARY

or

INTELLIGENCE SUMMARY.

(Erase heading not required.)

Instructions regarding War Diaries and Intelligence Summaries are contained in F. S. Regs., Part II. and the Staff Manual respectively. Title pages will be prepared in manuscript.

13TH BATTN EAST SURREY REGT.,
120TH BRIGADE,
40TH DIVN.

Place	Date	Hour	Summary of Events and Information	Remarks and references to Appendices
FONTAINE-CROISILLES SECTOR	25.XII.'17		Usual work in progress. ARTILLERY (our own and enemy's fairly active. Aeroplanes (Brit. and enemy) - normal activity. Patrols sent out by all Companies; nothing unusual occurred.	T.E.O. W.M.
Do	26.XII.'17		Usual work in progress. Artillery and aeroplane moderately active on both sides. Considerable enemy movement noted. Our snipers and L.G's registered hits. Patrols went out from Rt Centre, Left Centre and Left Companies' Sectors. Advanced Party of Officers & N.C.O's from the 11/ Suffolk Regt visited and reconnoitred the Sector.	W.B.O. W.M.
Do and ARMAGH CAMP, HAMELINCOURT	27.XII.'17		The Battn (and 1 Coy 11th R.LANCS. Regt.) were relieved by the 11th Suffolk Regt (101st Inf. Bgde) and 1 Coy. 10th Lincoln Regt (in support). Battn returned to ARMAGH CAMP.	W.M.O. W.B.O. W.M.
ARMAGH CAMP.	28.XII.'17		Day spent in clearing up and men bathed and were issued with changes of underclothing. The CO. and the Assist.Adjt visited new rest billets at DYSART CAMP. Recd from G.O.C.-120th Inf. Bgde:- Nº 120/4.21. "The G.O.C. is pleased that the observation from the East Surrey front was so good during yesterday (26th), and that the Sniping Secured Such Satisfactory Results"	W.B.O. W.M. W.B.O. W.M.

(Signed) H.B. Kerr - Capt.
A/Bgde Major.
27.XII.1917.

A5834 Wt.W4973 M68; 730,000 8/16 D.D. & L.Ltd. Forms/C.2118/13.

WAR DIARY
or
INTELLIGENCE SUMMARY.

(Erase heading not required.)

13th BATT'N EAST SURREY REG'r

120TH BRIGADE, 40TH DIVISION.

Instructions regarding War Diaries and Intelligence Summaries are contained in F. S. Regs., Part II. and the Staff Manual respectively. Title pages will be prepared in manuscript.

Place	Date	Hour	Summary of Events and Information	Remarks and references to Appendices
SOUTH CAMP, MORY.	29.XII. '17		The Batt'n moved from ARMAGH CAMP and went into Brigade Reserve - billeted in 12'8 CAMP, MORY - [B.22.c.9.4.] (ARMAGH CAMP was taken over by 7th K.S.L.I. - 8th Bgde, 3rd Div.) Batt'n marched via ERVILLERS. Capt. F.S.Beecroft proceeded on leave to ENGLAND.	Map 57 c. W.E.D. 2/Lt.
D°	30.XII. '17.		Day spent in cleaning up Camp and Equipment. Working party found for DYSART CAMP - constructing shelters in Transport Lines. The C.O. attended a conference of C.O's at Brigade A.Q. Notification of the following awards to the Batt° was received :- (a) D.S.O. :- Lt.-Col. H.L.WARDEN, (b) Military Cross :- Cpl. J.R.HUCKER, Capt. A.B.BURTON, 2/Lt. G.BEAUMONT, 2/Lt. W.B.PARKER. (c) Distinguished Conduct Medal :- N° 13121, Sgt. A.T.PIPER, N° 11981, Pte. R.S.FULLER.	W.E.D. 2/Lt.
D°	31.XII. '17		All Companies - S.B.Resp't inspection & drill. Otherwise Companies at disposal of O's C.Co'§. "A" Co' found two loading parties (R.E.) - one for BOYELLES; the other for DYSART CAMP. MAJOR W.G.T.KEDDIE and the O's C.Co'§ visited the new sector to reconnoitre. MAJOR W.G.WEST returned to duty from Senior Officers' Course, ALDERSHOT and took over the command of the Batt° - vice MAJOR W.G.T.KEDDIE.	W.E.D. 2/Lt.

W.G. West
[MAJOR]2

Commanding 13th Batt° East Surrey Reg't.

31st Dec., 1917.

A.5834. Wt.W.4973 M687. 750,000. 8/16 D.D.&L.Ltd. Forms/C.2118/13.

13th BATTN EAST SURREY REGT; **WAR DIARY**
OR
INTELLIGENCE SUMMARY

120TH BRIGADE, 40TH DIVISION.

December, 1917.

(Erase heading not required.)

Instructions regarding War Diaries and Intelligence Summaries are contained in F. S. Regs., Part II. and the Staff Manual respectively. Title pages will be prepared in manuscript.

Place	Date	Hour	Summary of Events and Information	Remarks and references to Appendices
Fontaine-Croisilles Sector.	12. XII.17		Casualties:- Killed: 2 O.Rs. Wounded:- Capt. J.R.HUCKER and 17 O.Rs.	W.G..D. H.C.
Do.	13/12/17		Wounded (Gas):- Capt. L.I.DEACON and 11 O.Rs.	W.G.D. H.C.
Do.	14/12/17		Wounded (Gas):- Lieut. S.Rutherford, 1 W.O. and 13 O.Rs. Wounded:- 5 O.Rs.	W.G.D. H.C.
Do.	16/12/17		Wounded (Gas):- 5 O.Rs.	W.G.D. H.C.
Do.	19/12/17		Wounded (Gas) - on 14th inst., but not previously reported:- 4 O.Rs	W.G.D. H.C.
Do.	26/12/17		Wounded:- 1 O.R.	W.G.D. H.C.

A5834   Wt. W4973/M687 750,000 8/16 D. D. & L. Ltd. Forms/C.2118/13.

Army Form C. 2118.

WAR DIARY

or

INTELLIGENCE SUMMARY.

(Erase heading not required.)

Instructions regarding War Diaries and Intelligence
Summaries are contained in F. S. Regs., Part II.
and the Staff Manual respectively. Title pages
will be prepared in manuscript.

Place	Date	Hour	Summary of Events and Information	Remarks and references to Appendices

CONFIDENTIAL.

20 D
10 sheet

WAR DIARY

for the month of

JANUARY, 1918.

15TH. BATTN. EAST SURREY REGT.,

120TH. INFANTRY BRIGADE,

40TH DIVISION.

VOLUME 20.

A5834 Wt. W4973 M687 750,000 8/16 D. D. & L. Ltd. Forms/C.2118/13.

WAR. DIARY
or
INTELLIGENCE SUMMARY.

(Erase heading not required.)

13TH BATTN EAST SURREY REGT.,
120TH INFANTRY BRIGADE, 40TH DIVISION.

Instructions regarding War Diaries and Intelligence Summaries are contained in F. S. Regs., Part II. and the Staff Manual respectively. Title pages will be prepared in manuscript.

Place	Date	Hour	Summary of Events and Information	Remarks and references to Appendices
Nº 8 CAMP, MORY. [B22c94.]	1.1.18		Parades under Coy Commanders – Physical Training with games and exercises. Inspections by Coy Commanders. Huts and lines cleaned up. "C" Coy found two working parties: (1.) 1 N.C.O. and 10 O.Rs at BOYELLES loading stabling material, (2.) 1 N.C.O. and 10 O.Rs at DYSART CAMP off-loading same. The C.O., the Adjutant and the Signalling Officer visited new sector to reconnoitre. Lieut. SIMONIS was sent to hospital.	MAP 57c. W.6.D. 7/6.1.
Dº and Left Sub-sector of NOREUIL Sector.	2.1.18		Early part of day spent in preparatory work and general cleaning-up of camp. The Battalion relieved the 11th Royal [LANCASHIRE] Regt. in Left Sub-sector of NOREUIL Sector. Relief completed by 9.45 p.m. Bn.H.Q. established at C.4.b.90.55. Fairly heavy hostile artillery & M.G. fire were experienced during the night. TANK AVENUE and HORSESHOE SUPPORT were enfiladed. Patrols sent out from RIGHT and RIGHT CENTRE COYS' fronts.	MAP: HENDECOURT. (1:20,000). W.6.D. 2/6.1.
Left Sub-sector of NOREUIL Sector.	3.1.18		Work in trenches in progress. Our artillery active throughout the day. Heavy hostile shelling (4.5"mms and 105"mms) between 12.30 and 1.30 p.m. HORSESHOE SUPPORT was damaged. TANK AVENUE proved a favourite target for M.G's. Considerable enemy movement was noted. A patrol was sent out in front of PUDSEY SUPPORT but was driven in by fire from T.M's.	W.6.D. 7/6.1.

A834   Wt. W.4973/M.687.   750,000.   8/16   D. D. & L. Ltd.   Forms/C.2118/13.

Army Form C. 2118.

WAR DIARY
or
INTELLIGENCE SUMMARY.
13th BATTN EAST SURREY REGT.,
120TH BRIGADE, 40TH DIVISION.

(Erase heading not required.)

Instructions regarding War Diaries and Intelligence Summaries are contained in F.S. Regs., Part II. and the Staff Manual respectively. Title pages will be prepared in manuscript.

Place	Date	Hour	Summary of Events and Information	Remarks and references to Appendices
	3.1.18.		(continued). The following new officers reported for duty and were posted to companies:- 2nd Lieut.s R.H. LAWRENCE, A.C. COWLING, E. SKIDMORE, O.P.OAKES, R.B.BISHOP, J.A.V.CANT.	W.E.O. etc.
Left sub-sector of NOREUIL Sector.	4.1.18.		Usual work in progress. Our Artillery was fairly active - particularly against PUDSEY SUPPORT and HENDECOURT. Enemy artillery was active - chiefly against our left front. Enemy aeroplanes dropped signals over our lines during the day. PATROLS went out from Rt Centre Coy's front to reconnoitre through U29a and obtain information re Enemy post in PUDSEY SUPPORT.	HENDECOURT. W.E.O etc.
Do.	5.1.18.		ENEMY RAID was made at 5.30 a.m. against sub-sector on our left. Some enemy bombs were thrown on our front but nothing else resulted. Enemy succeeded in obtaining footing in line on our Left- Sup (LONDON SUPPORT=U29a3588). Precautions - including establishment of blocks - were taken by our LEFT Coy- in HORSESHOE REDOUBT. Our artillery was active throughout the day. Hostile ARTILLERY was active at intervals during the day and night. TANK AVENUE vicinity of Batt.Q. was shelled between 5.30 pm and 9.30 pm.	W.E.O. etc.
Do.	6.1.18.		Artillery on both sides fairly active throughout the day. Battalion was relieved by the 11th ROYAL LANCS REGT and withdrew to support. Relief was completed by 10 p.m. B.H.Q. established at C10a 65.05.	W.E.O. etc.

A3534 Wt.W4973/M687 750,000 8/16 D.D. & L. Ltd. Forms/C.2118/13.

WAR DIARY

or

INTELLIGENCE SUMMARY.

(Erase heading not required.)

13TH EAST SURREY REGIMENT, 120TH BRIGADE, 40TH DIVISION.

Instructions regarding War Diaries and Intelligence Summaries are contained in F. S. Regs., Part II. and the Staff Manual respectively. Title pages will be prepared in manuscript.

Place	Date	Hour	Summary of Events and Information	Remarks and references to Appendices
Left Support, NOREUIL Sector.	7.1.18		Battalion in Support. Working parties found.	May /6
Do.	8.1.18		Usual work in trenches. Working party found for work on SIDNEY AVENUE.	May /6
Do.	9.1.18		Usual work in progress. Working party detailed for work as above. Capt. W.G. PRICE and 2/Lt M.H. ROWLAND proceeded on leave. 2nd Lieut. W.E. DOBB (B.I.O.) proceeded on leave to ENGLAND.	May /6
Do. and Left sub-sector NOREUIL Sector.	10.1.18		Battalion relieved the 11th ROYAL LANCS. REGT in left and b. sector. Relief completed at 7.45 pm. B.H.Q. established at C4b90.55. Patrols were sent out by the RIGHT coy. and the LEFT coy. Enemy M.G's active at U29b24. and U23 c 9.4. Our 18 pdrs were firing S.W. of RIENCOURT.	May /6
Left and b. sector NOREUIL	11.1.18	5 a.m.	Enemy shelled HORSESHOE SUPPORT with "mms". Usual work in progress in trenches. Two patrols were sent out to reconnoitre "NO MAN'S LAND" on Battn. front.	May /6
Do.	12.1.18		Hostile M.Gun at U29a7 was active. Our "heavies" shelled back areas — HENDECOURT, etc. LISTENING PATROLS were established in front of our wire and were out during hours of darkness.	May /6

A5534 Wt.W4973 M687 750,000 8/16 D.D.&L.Ltd. Forms/C2118/13.

Army Form C. 2118.

WAR DIARY
or
~~INTELLIGENCE SUMMARY.~~ 13TH BATTN EAST SURREY REGT.,
(Erase heading not required.) 120TH INF. BRIGADE, 40TH DIVISION.

Instructions regarding War Diaries and Intelligence
Summaries are contained in F. S. Regs., Part II.
and the Staff Manual respectively. Title pages
will be prepared in manuscript.

Place	Date	Hour	Summary of Events and Information	Remarks and references to Appendices
Left Sub-Sector, MOREUIL Sector.	13.1.'18		Hostile artillery shelled TANK AVENUE with 77mms during the morning. Our 60 pounders were employed (between 11 am and 2 pm.) in shelling in vicinity of U 23 c 7½. 18 pounders shelled RIENCOURT during the afternoon. Rather heavy hostile shelling of our front line was experienced during the night. 77mms and 10.5 m.ms were used. Enemy sent over gas-shells on C4d area (near Bttn H.Q.) between 8.30 & 9 pm. Two patrols searched "NO MAN'S LAND" on Battn. front - and found it clear of the enemy.	DCay
D° and N°8 Camp, MORY. (B22 c 94)	14.1.'18		The Battalion was relieved by the 11th ROYAL LANCASHIRE REGIMENT. Lieut. W. A. ANDREW returned to duty from sick leave. Lieut. J.F.M. MICHELMORE reported for duty. Notification was received that the VI Corps Commander would inspect the camp on the 15th inst.	DCay
MORY.	15.1.'18		Companies under Coy Commanders. Cleaning up in progress. The baths at MORY were allotted for the use of the Battn.	DCay
MORY.	16.1.'18		Parades etc. under Coy arrangements - Kit inspections, Inspection of S.B.R.'s, S.B.R. drill, etc. "A" Coy found working party of 1 Officer and 25 O.Rs. for work on new Assault Course at B 28 a 63. 2/Lieut. N.B. PARKER returned to duty from hospital	MAP. 57 c. DCay

A 534 Wt W4973/M687 750,000 8/16 D. D. & L. Ltd. Forms/C.2118/13.

WAR DIARY

or

INTELLIGENCE SUMMARY.

(Erase heading not required.)

13TH BATTN EAST SURREY REGT.,
120TH INF. BRIGADE, 40TH DIVISION.

Instructions regarding War Diaries and Intelligence Summaries are contained in F. S. Regs., Part II. and the Staff Manual respectively. Title pages will be prepared in manuscript.

Place	Date	Hour	Summary of Events and Information	Remarks and references to Appendices
	16.1.18		(continued) Lieut. D.E. BERNEY (of the U.S.M.R.C.) took over the duties of M.O. vice Lieut. R.D. MacGREGOR who proceeded on leave to ENGLAND. Capt. F.S. BEECROFT returned from leave and resumed charge of the Transport Section. Lieut. W.L. MALLET (acting Transport Officer) therefore returned to duty with "D" Coy. The C.O. inspected all Companies.	Diary
MORY.	17.1.18		Companies under Coy. Commanders. "C" Coy. found working party as for 16th inst. The M.O. inspects the feet of all O.R.s. Capt. C.E. LINGE proceeded to hospital.	Diary
MORY and left sector of NOREUIL sector	18.1.18		Battn. relieved the 11TH ROYAL LANCS. REGT. in left sub-sector, NOREUIL. B.H.Q. were established at C4.b.90.55. Listening patrols were posted on both Companies' fronts throughout the hours of darkness. Hostile Artillery & M.G's were fairly active throughout the night.	Diary
Do	19.1.18		Work on trenches in progress. Our Artillery did effective work against RIENCOURT and HENDECOURT areas. Hostile shelling of STONEY AVENUE and RAILWAY RESERVE during the night. Some E.A. activity between 11 a.m. and 12 noon. Listening Posts established in both Companies fronts. They remained in front of wire during darkness.	Diary

A5834 Wt. W4973 M687 750,000 8/16 D. D. & L. Ltd. Forms/C.2118/13.

WAR DIARY

or

INTELLIGENCE SUMMARY. 13TH EAST SURREY REGT.,

140TH INFANTRY BRIGADE, 40TH DIVISION.

(Erase heading not required.)

Instructions regarding War Diaries and Intelligence
Summaries are contained in F. S. Regs., Part II
and the Staff Manual respectively. Title pages
will be prepared in manuscript.

Place	Date	Hour	Summary of Events and Information	Remarks and references to Appendices
Left Sub-sector, NOREUIL Sector.	20.1.18		There was the usual activity by our Artillery, T.M's and M.G's. The enemy shelled TANK AVENUE, SYDNEY AVENUE and vicinity of Btn.Q. Listening posts were established on both Companies' fronts. 2/Lt. SIMPSON proceeded on leave to ENGLAND.	Aly
Do.	21.1.18		Our Artillery shelled RIENCOURT with 18 pounders. T.M's were employed against PUDSEY SUPPORT. The enemy's artillery was normal. RAILWAY RESERVE and the RIGHT Company's front were the chief targets— 77 mms and 105 mms being employed. 2/Lt. MOLENKAMP proceeded to hospital.	Aly
Do. and Left Support.	22.1.18		The Battalion was relieved in the left sub sector (NOREUIL sector) by the 11TH ROYAL WARCS. REGT and withdrew to left support position. Btn.Q. were established at C.10 a 6.5. 05.	Aly
Left Support NOREUIL sector.	23.1.18		In Support. Working parties were employed in work on Support trenches and SYDNEY AVENUE. Carrying parties were also found. Lieut. Col. H.L.WARDEN, D.S.O., returned from leave and resumed command of the Battalion.	Aly
Do.	24.1.18		In Support. Working parties and Carrying parties found as above (23rd inst.)	Aly

A5834   Wt. W4973 M687   750,000   8/16   D. D. & L. Ltd.   Forms/C.2118/13.

WAR DIARY

or

~~INTELLIGENCE SUMMARY.~~

(Erase heading not required.)

13TH BATTY EAST SURREY REGT,

120TH INFANTRY BRIGADE, 40TH DIVISION

Instructions regarding War Diaries and Intelligence Summaries are contained in F. S. Regs., Part II. and the Staff Manual respectively. Title pages will be prepared in manuscript.

Place	Date	Hour	Summary of Events and Information	Remarks and references to Appendices
Left Support, Left Sub-Sector, NOREUIL.	25.1.18		In sup't fort. Working parties, etc. found as on previous days.	W.D.
Left Sub-sector, NOREUIL.	26.1.18		The Batt'n relieved the 11th ROYAL LANCS. REGT. in left Sub-sector, NOREUIL. B.H.Q. established at Cubgo.55. Relief completed by 7.45 p.m. Disposition of Companies:- Rt. Front :- "D" Coy; Rt. Support :- {RAILWAY "B" Coy; Left Front :- "C" Coy; Left " " :- {RESERVE- "A" Coy. Our Artillery activities - normal. Enemy's artillery sent over gas-shells most of which fell near left Post of the Right Front Company. Patrols went out on both Companies' fronts. 2/Lt. W.E. DOBB (B.I.O.) resumed his duties on returning from leave.	W.B. ① 2/Lt.
D°	27.1.18.		Our artillery's activity normal throughout the day. A heavy mist prevailed during the day. Several of the enemy took advantage of this and came out into the open from which our SUPPORT to do salvage work. Our snipers caused their retirement. At 8 p.m. a lost S.O.S. barrage was fired in co-operation with the Division on our right. After this barrage, the enemy shelled our front line posts with 105 m'ms. and 77 m'ms. A PATROL went out from Rt. Co's front.	W.D. 2/Lt.

A5834 Wt. W4973/M687 750,000 8/16 D. D. & L. Ltd. Forms/C.2118/13.

Army Form C. 2118.

WAR DIARY
or
INTELLIGENCE SUMMARY. 13TH. EAST SURREY REGT.,
120TH. INF. BRIGADE, 40TH DIVISION.
(Erase heading not required.)

Instructions regarding War Diaries and Intelligence
Summaries are contained in F.S. Regs. Part II.
and the Staff Manual respectively. Title pages
will be prepared in manuscript.

Place	Date	Hour	Summary of Events and Information	Remarks and references to Appendices
Left Sub Sector, NOREUIL Sector.	28.1.18		Normal general activity by our Artillery. During the afternoon, 6" Hows & T.Ms. did effective work on BUNNY HUG LANE and PUDSEY SUPPORT. Our snipers were active. Enemy's artillery was particularly quiet. There was some E.A. activity during the morning and afternoon. E.A. Bombed back areas between 6.30 p.m. and 11 p.m. E.A. returned over our lines at 11 p.m. "A" & "B" Companies relieved "C" & "D" in front line. "C" and "D" companies withdrew to close support in RAILWAY RESERVE. One reconnoitred found in front of PUDSEY SUPPORT; the other two patrols went out. One reconnoitred "tank" at U29a66 was unoccupied. ascertained that derelict "tank" at U29a66 was unoccupied. Capt. F.S. AINGER (Adjutant) and Lieut. A.W. GILL proceeded on leave to ENGLAND.	W.S.D. Ht.
Do.	29.1.18		Our Artillery shelled U24c and U18d (HENDECOURT) areas; trenches S.W. of RENCOURT, BUNNY HUG LANE and STARFISH TRENCH. Our Snipers obtained hits. Enemy artillery did little except between 8.30 p.m. and 9.15 p.m. Snipers were rather active from PUDSEY SUPPORT. Patrol from Rt. Coy's front examined enemy's line from U29a77 to U29a99 35.	W.S.D. Ht.
Do. and N° 8 Camp, MORY.	30.1.18		Normal activity on both sides. Battalion was relieved by the 11th. ROYAL LANCS. REGT. Relief was completed by 7.30 p.m. The Battalion withdrew to Brigade Reserve at N° 8 Camp, MORY.	[B32c94 MAP: 57c.] W.S.D. Ht.

WAR DIARY
or
INTELLIGENCE SUMMARY.

13TH BATTN EAST SURREY REGT.

(*Erase heading not required.*)

120TH INF. BRIGADE, 40TH DIVISION.

Instructions regarding War Diaries and Intelligence Summaries are contained in F. S. Regs., Part II. and the Staff Manual respectively. Title pages will be prepared in manuscript.

Place	Date	Hour	Summary of Events and Information	Remarks and references to Appendices
Nº C Camp. MORY.	31.1.18		Companies under Company Commanders. Cleaning-up, etc. in progress. Working party was found by "D" Col.; work to render shelters at Brigade H.Q.	Wb.2.9.
			Bomb-proof.	What.
			The C.O. lectured to Junior Officers and N.C. O's on "Field Engineering."	
			Lieut. R.H. PEACOCK proceeded on leave to ENGLAND.	
			—— CASUALTIES during JANUARY, 1918. ——	
Left Sub-sector, MOREUIL.	5.1.18	——	Wounded:- 1 O.R.	Wb.2.9.
	6.1.18	——	Wounded:- 3 O.R.	What.
	10.1.18	——	Wounded:- 1 O.R.	
	11.1.18	——	Killed:- 1 O.R.; Wounded:- 2 O.R.	
	12.1.18	——	Wounded:- 2 O.R.	
	14.1.18	——	Killed:- 1 O.R.; Wounded:- 2 O.R.	
	23.1.18	——	Wounded:- 1 O.R.	
	27.1.18	——	Wounded:- 2 O.R.	
	28.1.18	——	Wounded:- 1 O.R.	
	30.1.18	——	Killed:- 1 O.R.; Wounded:- 2 O.R.	

Total Casualties:-

KILLED:- 3 O.R.

WOUNDED:- 17 O.R.

W. Wardie

(Lieut.-Colonel),

Commanding 13TH BATTN EAST SURREY REGT.

A534 Wt. W4973/M687 750,000 8/16 D. D. & L. Ltd. Forms/C.2118/13.

Lightning Source UK Ltd.
Milton Keynes UK
UKOW07f0346270716

279255UK00006B/59/P